SHARING

AN ANTHOLOGY

Published by the Antelope Valley Writers Association
Lancaster, CA 93535

DEDICATION

This anthology is dedicated to all of the members of the Antelope Valley Writers Association: past, current, and future. Continue to read, write, and support one another. And may you be ever inspired and amazed by the beauty of the high desert.

About the ANTELOPE VALLEY WRITERS ASSOCIATION

The Antelope Valley Writers Association (AVWA) is a non-profit literary group that is free and open to the adult public. Their primary belief is that everyone has a story to tell. Every person is a walking storybook full of wisdom, history, and imagination.

AVWA members are people who enjoy life in the amazing high desert of the Antelope Valley in Southern California. All have a love of writing and a desire to share their stories. In fact the group's motto is, "Words are meant to be shared," and that is exactly what these dedicated individuals do in weekly meetings in the Lancaster Community Center and in their yearly anthologies.

In 2013, the AVWA published its first anthology, *SOARING*, a collection of short stories, poems, and memoirs written by members of the group. The success of that anthology led to a second book in 2014, *AMAZING*, and started an annual tradition of AVWA anthologies. With the publication of *SHARING* the AVWA continues its support for the local community by dedicating funds from the sales of its anthologies to needy causes. Copies of all AVWA anthologies are available through the group or from Amazon.com.

About the *SHARING* Anthology

SHARING: an Anthology is the third collection of short stories, poems, memoirs, and essays published by the AVWA. This book showcases the talents of thirty writers who live in the high desert of Southern California, an area where the artists are as unique as their native Joshua trees. *SHARING* has something for everyone: heartfelt poetry; stories that are sad, funny, and inspirational; and some that range from scary to grisly.

This 2015 anthology truly reflects the diversity of California's Antelope Valley. The talented authors in this book have worldly backgrounds that span from Mexico to the Middle East. They hail from all walks of life: doctors, teachers, students, artists, business owners, counselors, aerospace employees, homemakers, firemen, ministers, and entertainers. All have a desire to write and to share their stories with you.

ACKNOWLEDGMENTS

The AVWA would like to thank the following people whose hard work and dedication made this anthology a reality:

- Patricia Alexander, an amazing artist as well as a talented writer, who is President of the AVWA. In addition to chairing the weekly meetings, she is always the ideal hostess – always there with her beautiful smile. Pat also provided the professional artwork of her late husband, V.S. Alexander, which provided a striking cover for this anthology.

- Gail Javadi, the Vice President of the AVWA, who managed to pull thirty diverse writers together to gather the stories and poems that are presented in this anthology.

- Mary Denning, who is Secretary of the AVWA. She keeps track of all meetings and activities with her dedicated record keeping. Mary's attention to detail keeps the group honest.

- Doreen Kennedy, for taking on the huge tasks of editing, formatting, and publishing this anthology.

About the COVER ARTIST:

The vibrant artwork on the cover of this year's anthology was created by V.S. Alexander, the late husband of AVWA President Patricia Alexander. Besides painting, he created artworks in mosaic and stained glass media. His artistic talents extended to writing, and one of his poems can be found on Page 179.

CONTENTS

PAT ALEXANDER 10
    October in Antelope Valley..10
    Fallen Petals 11
    To Forgive 11
    Stage-Door Johnnies 12
    Hurricane Ridge 17
DOROTHY BACHELOR..18
    Jack..18
ALICE HUDSON 22
    Gibraltar 22
    Adventures on the Rogue...24
    Well, That Sounds Like Fun! 25
    Cowboys..26
ROGER CHRISTIANSEN 27
    Our Little One..27
    Halloween 29
    Going Fishing...30
    Shakespeare Fun 31
    Life's a Ride 33
KATIE RYAN 34
    Blood Moon (An Excerpt) 34
    Before Cowboy Music...39
FLORIDA JOHNS...40
    The Three Airmen 40
    Pretty Lady...43
    A Weekend in Paris 43
ESPERANZA BELTRÁN 48
    Her House...48
RICHARD C. ELTON, M.D. 50
    Pressed Pants...50
    Heaven..51
    Good Dog Spot 52
    The TET Offensive..54
    The Berlin Wall 56
JOAN MCCURDY ELTON 58
    Drought 2015 58
    Memories of Maine..59
    Frenetic Feeding of Fantastic Finches....................................61

MARY DENNING.. 62
   Letters... 62
   An Uphill Journey.. 65
   October... 66
   Those Crazy Holidays 67
   A Letter to Santa.. 68
   Requiem for Nora 69
CARL BACHELOR... 70
   To Canada From Us.. 70
AARON LEWIS... 72
   Lost.. 72
   In the Blink of a Eye 73
   Puncture.. 77
CARMEN BETANCOURT.. 78
   Vacation Thriller... 78
ADRIANA ALEXANDER... 85
   Television.. 85
   The Living Dead... 86
   Beholder of Magic 87
   Montenegro 88
   Coyote Pack.. 89
   Intertwined 90
   Angel: A Song for Franco 90
WILMA WEBSTER.. 91
   The Lampoon.. 91
   Joy of Band-Aids 94
   Poor Johnny 96
   The Boxing Smoker 97
STEVE ORDWAY 99
   Auto vs. Pole.. 99
   Precious.. 101
   Chingaso 102
FRANCES SERESERES 104
   Little Bird... 104
   Diana's Dream 107
   Time (T I M E) 108
   Looking Out My Kitchen Window.. 109

ELAINE BROWN 110
   A Wife's Predicament...110
   Journey Through Autumn..116
DENISE DALO-SCHIPPER...118
   A Place for Mom 118
JACKIE L. CROSSWHITE SR. 123
   Who Me...123
   I.D. 123
   Little Jack 124
   Fading Marriage 125
   It Meant Everything...126
   My Sixth Grade Fan Club..127
JAMES F. WOOD...128
   Turning Point 128
   October View 129
   Letters From Amy 130
   Passing of a Quiet Meadow...133
   Zorro and The Lone Ranger..134
   Encounter With A Clay Prophet...135
LOIS WILK..136
   Alligator Hunt 136
   Hernando's Hideaway 138
   Handkerchiefs 140
LORETTA J. JONES..142
   The Unsolved Mysteries of Sylvia 142
DARLENE PRYOR 146
   Tamar...146
   Hidden in Plain Sight 147
   If I Asked You 148
   If I Could 149
   Life and Plum Trees 150
   They Said vs. He Said...152
   I Am Tamar 153
DARRELL MONTGOMERY...154
   Life at the End of the Tunnel..154
ERLINDA C. MOODY 156
   The Bride Doll 156
   The Ferry Boat Serenade 158
   The Wrath of Grapes 161

HILDA TARAZI 164
  Coming to America 164
MELINDA M. HUNTER 167
  Desert Diamonds 167
  The Fifth Jesus (An Excerpt) 168
DOREEN KENNEDY 174
  City Rain 174
  A Snow Story 175
  Borrowed Time 177
  Names 178
V. S. ALEXANDER 179
  Exile from Paradise 179

INDIVIDUAL COPYRIGHTS 180

PAT ALEXANDER

Born and reared in Buffalo, New York, and having lived in several U.S. states and in Europe, Pat Alexander is happy to call the Antelope Valley's high desert her home.

Pat is multi-talented. She is a visual artist as well as a published author, and has also worked in the entertainment industry. While living abroad she studied art in several European cities and has exhibited and sold her paintings worldwide. She was also a principal entertainer, singing and dancing for eight years with the Folies Bergere and other stage shows in Las Vegas.

Pat discovered her writing talent in California, where she began composing short stories and poetry which she published as a collection in her first book, *Pollywogs and Green Things Growing*. In October, 2015, she published her second book, a memoir of her Vegas days titled *A Las Vegas Showgirl: Stories and Photos*. She is currently working on two more projects: a sequel to her first book which will include her artwork, and a continuation of her memoirs.

OCTOBER IN ANTELOPE VALLEY

Billowing black and white clouds
propelled by the wind
are kissing the tops of mountains
surrounding our valley.
A cold front is pushing through,
The first of the season.
Turn on the furnace, change the filter.
Feel the comforting warmth
Soothing your bones.
Ah, this feels so good.
Hilda and Princessa are barking outside,
Begging to come into the house.
Sweet Rosie in the kitchen, meowing for food.
Rita, the amazing Amazon parrot,
screeches for attention. She speaks,
"Let's all hunker down and get cozy, folks."

FALLEN PETALS

Fallen petals, as drops of blood,

Shed for love of self.

Put them away forever,

Remember them no more.

New life springs from the Geranium,

Living, breathing,

Soft red petals on my window sill.

Dare me to stay,

To be brave,

To love once more.

TO FORGIVE

To reach out
with my heart and
accept all things as they are.

No wished for dreams,
but reality as it is.
My hope is eternal, I hold it close
in my mind and savor it.
I prepare with it for my next
adventure to come.

STAGE-DOOR JOHNNIES

Just like the stars that can be counted upon to appear in the night sky every evening, our stage-door Johnnies were ever present. They would send large flower arrangements backstage to their favorite Las Vegas showgirl, in hopes that she may deign to allow them to take her out to dinner, or just to express their admiration for the girl of their dreams. Older men's hearts became young once again and quickened their beat with amorous thoughts. Young men's thoughts, always amorous, were even more so.

Sometimes a girl would get a phone call backstage and it turned out to be the wife of one of the star-struck Johnnies. For whatever reason, he couldn't resist telling his spouse about meeting a real live showgirl or dancer. The poor wife would get really upset and decide to call the lady in question and plead with her to leave her husband alone.

Of course, the showgirl he mentioned to his wife didn't even remember his name. He was just one of many admirers. So she would simply tell the stricken wife not to worry; her husband will get over it.

Darby Cline was one such admirer. He was an oil man from Texas who loved to play blackjack. He came to Las Vegas frequently looking forward to the turn of the cards. It didn't matter if he won or lost. It was the play that mattered. Missy Cline, his wife of forty plus years, never accompanied him as she didn't care for gambling.

He liked to stay at the Tropicana Hotel and play blackjack in their casino. The pit boss treated him right and kept the Jack Daniels flowing, on the house. One night Darby decided to see the Folies Bergere stage show in the Tropicana Hotel. He was such a favored player that Fred, the casino manager, gave him free access to the dinner show, food included.

Darby couldn't take his eyes off the lead showgirl descending the stairs on the main stage. Tall and slender with a slight tan that set off her yellow spangled costume trimmed in egret feathers. She had long blonde hair under a very tall plumed headdress and large expressive blue eyes that twinkled as she smiled, displaying perfect white teeth in a heart-shaped face.

What a stunner, he thought. She was the most exquisite woman he had ever seen in his life. He watched as she took her place on the stage between two dark haired beauties. His heart beat faster as he imagined her having dinner with him. Just the thought of the nearness of her caused him to be flustered and set his pulse racing and his brow perspiring. Maybe his friend, Fred, could introduce him to her.

He couldn't wait until the show ended and left the room to look for his buddy. Fred told him that he would arrange a meeting with the girl of his dreams, named Irene Taylor, as soon as possible. Fred could see how smitten Darby was with her. "Hang on Darby and after the show you will meet Irene in the lounge. Ask for Nick Marco, the manager, and he will seat you."

Irene was changing into her Finale costume with the expert help of Mary, a wardrobe lady, as there was little time between acts. It wasn't easy to put on the red velvet bikini bottomed, long flowing skirt with all the gold braid scrolled upon it, and also balance a heavy, towering hat with golden sequins etched on the red velvet material. Large sprays of golden raindrops edged the headdress and spilled over the rim. A lovely flowing white feathered cape completed the costume.

As the pipers in the Scottish band played the Finale music, Irene swept onstage and swirled her cape as she took her place down front, right above Darby who was sitting at a ringside table. Darby's face turned a bright shade of red as he beheld his dream woman in such close proximity. She glanced at him and smiled. As the trumpets sang out their final notes, the curtain came down and Darby hurried to the lounge to secure a table before Irene arrived. He sent four dozen roses back stage to her.

After they were introduced to one another, Nick left them alone at the table. "I want to thank you for the lovely roses," she said. "That was very sweet of you and thoughtful. But I must tell you that I am doing this as a favor to the bosses here as I don't usually mix with the customers."

Irene spoke with a beautiful, modulated voice – soft without any discernible accent. She was even more exquisite looking in person, thought Darby. His mind raced ahead to scenes of himself with Irene at some distant exotic locale with the two of them holding hands and gazing at the seashore and the gently lapping waves.

13

He caught himself daydreaming and said, "I really enjoyed watching you on the stage and thought perhaps you would care to have dinner with me. I don't want you to think that I have any ulterior motives. Is that all right with you?"

Irene thought, "Well, why not, he looks harmless enough."

He was a man's man type, about sixty years old. His hair was gray; he dressed well. His eyes were light blue with friendly wrinkles at the corners. A Southern accent completed her assessment of him.

"You don't mind having dinner right here in the Gourmet Room, do you, Darby? You see, I must get backstage to get dressed for the late show. I am sorry that I don't have more time but that's showbiz." She smiled at him and his heart thumped in his chest.

"Whatever you say, Irene. I just want to get to know you. I would like us to be friends so please look at me as a fan of yours, actually your biggest fan. I would never do anything to jeopardize our friendship, believe me."

He escorted her to the Gourmet Room for a great dinner of filet of sole with a fantastic mushroom sauce. "This is my favorite dish of all time, Darby, and I hope you enjoy it as much as I do." They gazed happily into each other's eyes as they polished off their food with some white wine.

"I'll be staying over this weekend, Irene, so I do hope you will go out with me again. I know some good restaurants we can try." They were already content with their meal and proceeded with small talk until Irene rose to leave to rejoin the show for the next performance.

"Here is my phone number, Darby. Call me tomorrow. We have rehearsals, but I'll see if I have the time to see you. I think you are a nice guy or I would never give you my number. Thank you for the delicious dinner."

After Darby met with Irene over the next few days he couldn't get her out of his mind. He tried to think of other things but he was enchanted. "What am I thinking?" he asked himself. "I've been a married man for many years. I love my wife and children."

But this girl had taken his fancy like no other in his life. Darby just had to court her and have her no matter what the cost. He would go slowly in this relationship as he didn't want to spook her. One thing he had learned in life was to be patient and all good things would eventually come your way. He began making plans to return to Vegas as soon as possible.

Irene was in the dressing room when Al, the stage manager, knocked on the door.

"Hey honey, you just hit the jackpot!" Al declared. "There is a big surprise waiting for you out in front of the hotel. You better hurry and go see before it disappears like in a magic trick."

Irene threw on her slacks and blouse and walked quickly to the front of the casino and out the big glass doors. The doorman approached her and handed her some car keys.

"A gentleman said this was for you," he said as he pointed to a beautiful white Pontiac convertible waiting by the curb and wrapped with a huge red bow. Irene couldn't believe her eyes.

"Are you sure, Peter? What gentleman are you talking about?"

"Well, a gray haired man with a Southern accent delivered the car and told me it was for you. Then he just disappeared into the night."

"Oh, I know who it is Peter. Thank you for letting me know what he looked like." She took the keys, got into the driver's seat and zoomed away for a ride.

"Gee what am I going to do about this?" she thought. "I can really use the car as my old jalopy is on its last legs. I never should have mentioned all of the problems I am having with my car. But hey, how many men would give you a new convertible? I will call Darby and tell him that I can't accept it. It is too much of a gift. Flowers or dinner are a different thing. Boy, he really must be crazy about me."

"Please Darby, it is just impossible for me to accept your gift," Irene spoke over the telephone. "I don't deserve a new car from you. I haven't agreed to be your girlfriend or anything like it. Please come here and take it with you."

He was pleading with her on the other end of the line to just take it in stride and use the car for awhile until she gets hers fixed. He didn't want her to feel obligated. After much conversation and reassurances he agreed to retrieve it.

Irene said, "Well alright Darby, but promise when you come back to Vegas you will take it, okay?"

And that is how Irene got to tool around in a brand new car, at least for the time being.

A few nights later before the first show, Irene was called to the phone backstage. "It's for you Irene," said Tony, the boy singer, as he handed her the phone.

A woman's voice was sobbing on the other end. She identified herself as Missy Cline, Darby's wife, and proceeded to tell a long story about her husband and his other dalliances in the past.

She said that he had told her about Irene and that he was in love and wanted a divorce. She pleaded with Irene to please give him up as he was the only true love of her life and she would just die without him. They had been married for forty-two years and this was what it had come to.

"Oh, Mrs. Cline, I am so sorry. I didn't realize the terrible hurt this was causing you. I just had dinner with him a few times but it was never any more serious than that. Here in Las Vegas men become enamored of the girls in the shows but we never take them seriously. I would never dream of breaking up your marriage and you can tell him I said so. As a matter of fact, tell him that I never want to see him again, ever."

The poor sad soul at the other end of the line breathed a sigh of relief, and thanked Irene for listening to her tale of woe.

"You can be sure, Irene, that Darby will never bother you again or he will have his children to answer to, not to mention my lawyer." With that said she hung up and to this day Irene never heard from either of them again.

And as she drove around enjoying her new car, with the top down and the desert wind blowing her hair into the soft, night breeze, Irene mused about the stage-door Johnnies and the passions of men. Whether young or old they can't resist beautiful showgirls.

HURRICANE RIDGE
(The Olympic Peninsula)

I cried at the top of the mountain
Beholding the beauty awaiting us there
Deer by the roadside nibbling on wild greens
Lifting their noble heads at our approach
Keepers of old secrets the mountain holds dear.

Hurricane Ridge it is named
Throngs of tourists were there
From many different lands they came to see
To worship at the mountain peak
Some even hiked up the trail

A Marmot jumps up and chatters
The rodent is plentiful here
He looks like a pudgy weasel
With his dense golden hair

Five Blue Grouse dance by in front of our car
A mama bird with half grown babies
All chubby without any fear

Winding pathways on the road
Leading us ever upwards
Wow! What a view we saw from here

Mountains marching into infinity
Dense green fir trees alive on their flanks
Look towards the Sea and the fantastic beaches
Awaiting us there - with the great
Mother of all oceans - the wide wonderful blue Pacific

Ah, the mountains, the mountains
We twice ascended the twisting turning trail
We had to see once again such a mighty magic place
A place to dwell, a place to remember
For all ways. For keeps.

DOROTHY BACHELOR

Dorothy Bachelor, a native New Yorker, had four of her eight children in New York and four were born in California. Most women would choose to relax after raising such a large family, but not Dorothy. In addition to being a true female pioneer as one of the first women to work on the assembly of the Space Shuttle, she went to college and received a B.A. in Social Studies when she was 61 years young.

Dorothy is a long time member of the Antelope Valley Writers Association. Her writing endeavors include a column for a company newspaper and letters to the editor of the local Antelope Valley newspaper which have been published often. She has also written stories for small children, is currently working on a book which is a collection of essays, and another collection of stories on people in the aerospace industry. Dorothy resides in Lancaster, CA, and is happily married to her husband of forty-two years.

JACK

I'm going to de-moan Jack. I'm going to de-wail Jack. A bright, tangy day awaits me and I face wails and moans berating my ears.

Old age is beautiful but quirky. I cannot hear some of the important stuff on TV but I can hear Jack moaning and wailing through the closed double glass doors, through the closed bedroom door, and under the blankets. He has a moan that would do a graveyard credit. He has a wail that would have cars pulling over to the side if I turned him loose on the freeway. All he wants is to be IN. He wants to be at the center of attention - in the house, under your feet, in your face, around people (children preferably) - but IN all the time. He is a black and white, furry, hair-shedding, forty-five pound collection of solidified love. The dog is nuts. All he wants is to be touched, loved, talked to, and AROUND. He also is a heavy stepper on your bare feet, which he does frequently. It wears on the nerves, sometimes.

Jack has phenomenal hearing. If he is zonked out on the hall floor (the better to track which way I'm going in the house), he can

18

hear me unwrap a Milky Way bite-size candy about twenty feet away. First his eyes open, and he zeroes in on where I am. If I'm standing in the kitchen, he knows I'm fooling around with food. Then his ears sort of twitch to an all-alert position. The tail starts to wave a little, at the tip only. Next thing, this dog is sitting at my feet, tail going full tilt, eyes staring into my soul, head up in a pleading position, waiting –waiting for his piece. Drives me nuts!

But Jack is just pure love. He loves people. He gets a little picky about other four-footed furry things although he tolerates Miss Kitty, our striped matriarch, and he absolutely cares for Penny, our other little furry person. He grooms Penny and cares for her, plays with her, lets her jump up and bring him down when they're playing, but when it comes to eating that's a whole 'nother story.'

Jack will eat almost anything I hand him, and he has to have his first. Then it's okay to let Penny have hers, but Jack first. He will eat dog food if it isn't beef-based. Chicken, turkey, okay, but not beef. I wonder if he knows something we don't. Jack will ignore dry dog food and eat grass instead. But he will eat dry cat food. He can be tricked by a liberal application of shredded cheese on almost anything, but once the cheese is gone, so's Jack.

We have this routine in the morning: I open the patio room door, let Jack and Penny into the house, then we go out the front door to get the morning paper. Jack and Penny run down the block, check out previously checked-out bushes and mailboxes, come back, run around the circle, and then back into the front patio. Jack likes to see how far down the block he can go without my calling him and getting upset if he doesn't come right back, sort of like a child testing his limits. When he does come, it sounds like a small pony galloping at about thirty mph, and I often think, "If he misjudges and barrels into me at this rate, I'm dead meat." But, with some uncanny, radar-like sense, he stops just before hitting me. If he feels frisky, he'll look up at me from the corner, wag his tail, and turn around and keep going just to tease me.

One wintry morning he did this and I had no patience for games that day, having to take my grandson to school. I had to leave at a certain time and there was no getting away from it. Jack was teasing me and I had to say, "Okay, I'll take care of you when I get back!" I took my grandson to school, fully expecting Jack to be sitting next to Penny at the front door when I returned.

Penny was a goody-two-shoes when she sensed I was perturbed with Jack. When I returned, sure enough, there sat Penny at the front door looking as though she should be wearing a halo, but her rascally companion was nowhere in sight. I roamed the neighborhood, the neighboring neighborhoods, and the whole darn town. I couldn't spot Jack.

Well, I had to go pick my grandson up at school so I broke off the search for Jack. Actually, I thought, "Good. Good riddance. Go put yourself in someone else's face, shed fur all over their house, and pester them into frustration for a change. It'll be a relief not to have to sidestep your morning charge into the house; I'm sick of you trampling on my feet."

Next morning, I was devastated to realize that Jack really wasn't there. I didn't believe I could miss him so darn much. The whole day, and no Jack.

That night I dreamed about him. I saw him lying on a lawn in the corner of two cement block walls nearby. The next morning, I took my grandson to school and on the way home, decided to reconnoiter the same territory I'd been over a dozen times already. There he was sitting in a corner of two walls, on property right around the corner from our block about two blocks away. I parked the car and jumped out and ran towards him calling him and patting my knees. He sort of stared at me and then when I got real close a look of recognition came into his eyes, and he bounded into my arms, almost knocking me over. He jumped right into the car, and we went happily home.

I realized then that Jack didn't see too well. I also realized Jack and Penny both were aging. It finally dawned on me that maybe I'd better look at my furry friends as a little less furry and more just plain friends. They must have deteriorating senses and muscles, too! When that realization set in, I'm sure I made their lives a lot more comfortable. Jack has conceded that he doesn't have to be "in my face" all the time, just underfoot and around. It seemed right, somehow, to share the journey with Jack and Penny and Miss Kitty, because they're moving a little slower these days, as am I, and they rise a little more creakily, so to speak, as do I. Their eyes are a little dimmed. I can identify with that. I can't read for as long as I used to. But, when things slow down, when strength wanes, time allows more love and warmth to seep in, filling up the gaps and balancing the losses. I listen now for Jack's moans and wails.

July 4, 1999 - Miss Kitty died.

December 7, 1999, Jack was euthanized in my arms, in our home, cancer having almost consumed him - his leg, his lungs. Miss Penny is almost over her grieving now, a little perkier than she was immediately following Jack's demise. She follows me around like a shadow. I don't mind a bit. I miss Jack. He was my friend. I miss Miss Kitty. She was our reigning Princess. I'm too old now to engage in any more relationships with furry friends. They'd most likely out-live me and then where would they be? Who'd care for them? But I'll tell you something - I wish I could still hear Jacks moan and Jack's wail, and I wish Miss Kitty were here to walk across the page of the book I'm reading.

Epilogue:

Penny died the following year. I'm without my faithful companions but I have a challenge remaining. A stray cat that we had captured in a cat trap and taken to the Vet's to have neutered, hangs around. I've tried to capture it again to offer it up for adoption, free, as I did other strays but this one is too smart. She will not be caught. She actually enters the trap, consumes the bait and exits the trap, carefully avoiding the trigger. Very clever, this cat, and extremely jumpy. I guess I would be too, after being trapped, operated on and let free. After a few unsuccessful attempts to capture her, I just put a bowl of the cheapest dried cat food out in the patio room and a bowl of water. She would eat and drink and walk around near me, but if I made a move, she'd take off like a streak of greased lightning. This relationship lasted almost two years, until finally this cat let me touch her. Another year and she would jump up onto the swing bench next to me and eventually onto my lap. She learned to utilize the pet door so I moved her food dish and water into the house.

We've established a routine now, and I enjoy her, but my deep love for Jack and Penny and Miss Kitty prohibit my getting any closer to her than I am now, which is to be sure she has food and water and some petting. After all, she is aging too, and there is nothing that is needed with age, as much as a gentle touch, a little love, and someone to care.

21

ALICE HUDSON

Alice Hudson is a native Californian and a graduate of Chapman University. She has resided in several West Coast locations but now calls the Antelope Valley her home. Her various adventures, humorous experiences, and passionate interests in amateur stage and the arts have formed the basis for her yearning to write about laughter and life.

She and her husband have been married for fifty-five years and have owned and operated a Hallmark store for twenty-seven years, which contributes even more material for her writing. Alice loves to laugh as does her family: a daughter, son-in-law, and two grandsons. She hopes her writing will continue to capture the humor and laughter that have been so important to her.

GIBRALTAR

Didn't everyone grow up recognizing, "solid as the Rock of Gibraltar?" Well, it may not be as solid as one might think! Visiting the Rock was an incredible experience for my husband and me.

Riding a tour van from the city of Gibraltar up the rocky slopes, we stopped to see the 230-plus monkeys that call the Rock home. Yes, monkeys! Many years ago the monkeys hitched a ride on a boat from Morocco on the African continent, which can be seen across the straits from the Rock. There is an interesting legend that if the monkeys ever disappear from the Rock, the area will revert back to Spain, which it is physically attached to. Great Britain has claimed the area since 1713.

We have no doubt it will remain British. One of the monkeys actually entered our van and sat on the lap of one of our group before jumping to a packsack left behind by another of our group who had exited the van to take pictures. The monkey was adept at opening the packsack and removing food articles to take with it as we shooed it out of the van.

At the next stop, we donned multicolored hard hats for an excursion to the interior of the Rock. During WWII there were thirty-two miles of tunnels dug out of the Rock. Some of the tunnels were large enough for military personnel trucks to traverse the caves. As we walked a portion of the tunnels we observed large areas that had been used as cafeterias, hospitals, men's and women's sleeping dormitories and work rooms all carved out of the hard rock.

During WWII the Nazis observed the activity in the area as the Rock was a strategic location controlling the shipping into and out of the Mediterranean. Large gun emplacements guarding that passage are still there. The material dug out of the rock during the day was moved out under cover of darkness. It went to a local rock quarry which was mined during the day to hide the activity within the Rock from the observing Nazis. The Germans never suspected what was going on inside.

Believe it or not, Dwight Eisenhower, Franklin Roosevelt, and Winston Churchill held meetings within the Rock. At one point near the end of our walk through the Rock we had to split up our group as the path shrunk. Our imaginations traveled back to the 1940s. In this setting it seemed like only yesterday. Passing through a narrow 180 degree cleft, we emerged onto a hanging shelf on the rear of the rock that was high up the vertical cliff and overlooked the Gibraltar airport far below. We watched planes landing on the treacherous air strip that extends to the shore of the Mediterranean. There is a major highway bisecting the runway and when a plane lands or takes off, the highway is shut down. The airport is on the list of the ten most dangerous airports in the world.

As we left Gibraltar and headed into the Mediterranean, the captain of our cruise ship chose a point facing the east side of the Rock to cut the engines and drift for a period of time. We were able to experience the serenity of the water and the amazing sight of the whole of the Rock in surreal silence. Gibraltar's history and sights have added so much color to our travels. That "big rock" remains one of our favorite memories.

ADVENTURES ON THE ROGUE

"Fish on! Watch out! Coming through!"

The shouts of the fishermen alerted the other boats that something was up.

It was another glorious day at the mouth of Oregon's Rogue River at the peak of the salmon run upriver. The lucky fishermen had hooked an enormous salmon that was giving them a run for their money. Unfortunately, the commotion had attracted a hungry seal.

Picture if you will, two fishermen hanging on for dear life, one of whom had rod in hand as their boat was speeding around the bay chasing a lovely hooked salmon which was in turn being pulled away by a seal which was also fishing for dinner. Eventually the hapless fisherman was forced to cut the line, giving in to the seal, much to the relief of the surrounding fisher folk in their boats.

You are a different world away when you're on the Rogue. Peaceful, yet turbulent, the river and its shoreline draw wildlife such as bears, deer, otters, bald eagles, ospreys and water ouzels or dippers. Zane Grey, the famous author of western-themed novels, had a summer cabin alongside the river.

For adventure, you can take the jet boat up the river. If you prefer not getting wet, don't. However, fishing is king, particularly in the fall.

Much to my surprise, my husband and his buddy actually asked me to join them on the fishing boat! We knew our guide quite well. I promised not to talk too much. Wouldn't you know it; I got the first bite and set the hook. As the guys gave me room to play the fish and our guide maneuvered his boat, I couldn't believe the fighting strength of an "iddy-biddy" Chinook salmon.

I was proud to land the twelve-pound fish (with a little help from the guide and a net). The salmon was flopping around on the deck under the net, so I placed one foot on each side of the fish. Our patient guide quietly suggested to me that the salmon wasn't going anywhere, and that I really didn't need to stand on his net.

WELL, THAT SOUNDS LIKE FUN!

"It beats the monotony of lap swimming."

So spoke the members of our local competitive swim team. The plan was to participate in a competitive ocean swim in Santa Monica, California. Older swimmers, thirteen and up, could enter with a buddy. The course started from the beach, went out to a buoy, turned south or parallel to the beach past the end of the Santa Monica pier to another buoy, and then turned back to shore, all against the clock.

Our daughter and her devoted girlfriend signed up. They needed a guardian to swim nearby on a surfboard, just in case. So, I thought, why not me? I love to swim and I was strong.

"Bang" sounded the starting pistol and hundreds of healthy young swimmers and their guardians hit the surf. Our girls were swimming very well. Our daughter, a long distance freestyler, was guiding her pal who was swimming the backstroke.

Meanwhile, I was rapidly becoming aware that I wasn't made to be a surfboarder. I was sometimes on the nine-foot surfboard and mostly off it in the water. I had definitely bitten off way more than I could chew. Out of the ocean appeared an adorable young junior lifeguard on his surfboard who offered, very politely, to tow me to the beach. My stubbornness took over and I said, "I'll let you know – thanks." At that point my foot was nudged by something – maybe a friendly dolphin or something else.

That did it. I called out to my wonderful junior lifeguard, and he helped me navigate to the beach by towing me close to the breaking surf where I could finish by myself. My poor husband and daughter and the rest of our swim group offered me warm towels. Gradually my lips made the return from blue to pink as I was made to drink lots of steaming hot chocolate. Not too embarrassing!

Little did I know then, but many years later my two grandsons would spend many of their summers as junior lifeguards in Long Beach, California, rescuing little old ladies from the ocean.

Oh, one more fact: that summer of 1974 was when *Jaws*, the movie, came out!

COWBOYS

It was another glorious mountain morning at North Lake Tahoe. There's nothing like it. Brilliant blue sky, breathtaking peaks, clear-as-a-bell water and chilly air – a perfect morning to have a chuck wagon Western breakfast on the Ponderosa Ranch.

The six of us decided that it would be great fun to visit the set of *Bonanza*, the very popular television series. The three of us ladies rode a hay wagon with breakfast makings up the hill where we were met with steaming cups of coffee laced with bourbon, also known as BBB – Bourbon Before Breakfast. Talk about warming up in a hurry!

Soon we heard the clip-clopping of horses as they came up the hill on the other side of the arroyo. Sure enough, our husbands appeared dressed as cowboys astride horses from the wild, Wild West.

One of the fellows sneezed continuously, as he was allergic to his horse named Killer. Bob rode a horse named Buttons and as we yelled out, "Hi, Bob," Buttons came to an abrupt stop and refused to take another step. Well, that did it. Our husbands dismounted and headed for the BBB.

We were treated to a huge chuck wagon breakfast of juice, eggs, hotcakes, bacon and sausage, and lots of hot coffee with bourbon. The cowboy husbands elected to ride the hay wagon back down the hill, foregoing the horse ride. However, we ladies were very proud of our husbands' attempts to be cowboys!

ROGER CHRISTIANSEN

Roger Christiansen is a retired civil maintenance supervisor from the California Department of Water Resources. He has lived in the Antelope Valley since 1977.

Roger sings, plays guitar and ukulele, and has decided to try his hand at writing. He recently joined the Antelope Valley Writers Association to hone his writing skills.

OUR LITTLE ONE.

Into each life, some rain must fall

and you tell we get it all

but darlin' dear with you I disagree

you stand there getting wet

saying the worst ain't over yet

But tell me, how much better can it be?

Cause we have our little one

such joy and such fun

his gift of mirth and merriment

is only something heaven sent.

Our little boy, who sets our hearts a Joy

Tell me how much better can it be?

27

There's bill collectors at our door
we gave 'em some money, but they still want more
the telephone don't have a dial tone.
We're getting letters in the mail
from folks who want to put me in jail
but right now we have us a happy home.

Cause we have our little one
such joy and such fun
his gift of mirth and merriment
is only something heaven sent.
Our little boy, who sets our hearts a Joy
Tell me how much better can it be?

I've had it, it's been a bad day
and everything has gone the wrong way
yes everything is closing in on me dear.
then you say look up in the sky
and though you see the clouds on high
you should know the rainbow ends right here.

Cause we have our little one
such joy and such fun
his gift of mirth and merriment
is only something heaven sent.
Our little boy, who sets our hearts a Joy
Tell me how much better can it be?

HALLOWEEN

A long time ago when I was about ten or eleven years old, on Halloween our school used to have all the kids wear their costumes and parade around the playground. It was always a good time to be unique with your costume.

At that time a few science fiction movies were playing at the theater and I got the idea to be a robot. Nobody I knew had even thought of it in my neighborhood. So I got cardboard boxes, one for the chest and a smaller one for my head. I painted my old sneakers silver and made sleeves and pant legs out of silver plastic material. I cut out eye holes in the smaller box and cut out arm holes in the larger box. Then I glued old radio knobs and dials on the front of the chest box. I had painted both boxes silver, too. So when I put them all together, the silver boxes, silver painted shoes and silver plastic fabric fashioned into sleeves and pant legs, I looked like a robot, to me anyway.

A friend of mine came over and when he saw what I did, he decided to copy mine and wear his, too. It was my idea, but he did his pretty much like I did mine. I probably shouldn't have cared, but he shouldn't have taken my original idea and copied it.

Well on Halloween night I went trick or treating from my house. When I got in front of the house of an old grouchy man we called "Crab Apple" I started up the walkway and realized that he wasn't going to be happy or have any candy for me. So I stopped and grabbed the bottom of my graffiti bag, full of lots of shredded paper, and spun around and broadcast the bag's contents all over his lawn.

Just then I heard someone yelling and coming from out of the shadow of his front porch. He chased me, but I ran as fast as I could and got away. A little while later, my friend left his house and was coming from the other direction, hitting every house including Crab Apple's. Well old Crab Apple caught my friend when he came up the walkway to his house. He made him pick up every bit of graffiti that I had earlier coated his lawn with. Later, when he told me what happened, we knew it was I who was the guilty party. But I didn't really feel guilty. I just couldn't help but feel like justice had been served for him stealing my original idea.

GOING FISHING

"Going fishing," that is what I call the peaceful restful times I manage to carve out of my former hectic days. The "going fishing" I am talking about is sort of like if you went fishing, but not to catch a fish, so you didn't need any bait. No bait - no need for a hook. No hook - is there really any need for fishing line? You really don't even need a pole, to be going fishing, because it is a state of mind and it is as stress free as it can be.

I could sit by the aqueduct at lunch time and enjoy the peacefulness of the moment, no need to be involved in anything but the moment itself. Another way I could be "going fishing," was when I would pick up my guitar and all my cares just fell by the wayside. The weight melted right off of my shoulders as I managed to lose myself in the music. Whether I was trying to figure out some tune or playing one I already knew, or even 'noodling' (playing for exercise or playing groups of notes almost unconsciously) it was still like a "gone fishing" experience to me.

My hope is that everyone realizes, and that they may find, they have a "going fishing" activity that they can experience. Painting, writing, sculpting, inventing, or whatever takes their minds off of their stress. Lately, I have heard it is also called "going to your happy place." So I hope the next time your cares start to stress you out that you might seek out your "happy place" and "go fishing." You don't even need a license.

SHAKESPEARE FUN

My daughter asked, "Daddy, do you like Shakespeare?"

I said, "No, I don't know anything about him and I don't understand how he talks."

Then (a long time later), a very gifted lady came to our writers meeting. She offered us seniors, who had many life experiences, to consider joining an eight week class, meeting every Friday, to learn about acting out some monologues from some of Shakespeare's plays.

I decided to try. I could always stop. All others in the class had acted parts in his plays at one time or another, mostly during their younger college years. All seemed to know about his plays except for me.

I made it clear that I wasn't familiar at all with Shakespeare. I didn't understand how he talked and was confused about exactly what we were going to learn. The teacher assigned an act and a part to me and shared a book with my monologue in it. On one side of the page were Shakespeare's words and on the opposite page were the meaning of his words in today's language. This was really a great help to me.

We all studied our lines and rehearsed them every Friday, with our goal of putting on a "Shakespeare Showcase" for the folks at the Senior Center. During that time, I truly discovered Shakespeare and gained a great respect for his humor, wit, and romantic writings.

The romantic speech by Romeo was so descriptive, I found myself wondering if I could have ever said it better than he did? I think not. In *King Lear*, the king challenging the thunderstorm was so descriptive and conveyed such a final defeated blow against him that I marveled at Shakespeare's talent to write. The audience shares in the final defeat and identifies with the anger at the elements, assaulting the once noble king.

The comedy *The Merry Wives of Windsor* is about a false letter sent to a man, and he thinks his wife is cheating on him. How he shares his dismay and wrongful conclusion with the audience is also very entertaining.

The hidden gem was the teacher. What a storehouse of talent and training. We were so fortunate to have such a talented person opening up the many facets of Shakespeare, and guiding us to understand it and directing us to do it with our own interpretations based on our own life experiences.

I recommend an acting class in Shakespeare, like the one I attended, for anyone who wants to have fun and for anyone who thinks Shakespeare is over their head. It was a special life experience in itself and I will never forget it.

LIFE'S A RIDE

I see life as entering onto a ride in a fun house, at the end are two doors and that is where we exit. Many are aging as fast as I am and some have rushed ahead and got out through the door before me. I miss them and their wonderful ways that made them so unique.

I wonder if I am rushing, too, or should I relax and enjoy the trip as much as I can? I wonder to myself, how many songs have I got left and how many summers will I pass through before I get to that door? I really can't tell, so I am going to sing as many songs as I can and enjoy as many seasons as I can, until I reach that door.

During my ride, I have found out there are two doors and there is one I really don't want to go through. There was a time when the car I was in was going to go through that door, so I jumped off onto the car that was not going there. It was such a close call that I almost missed it.

So now, before I reach the right door, I will use this time to try to convince my former fellow riders to jump to safety before they reach the wrong door and it is too late for them. If we fellow riders all yell together, we can get everyone's attention, and they will hear us and jump.

KATIE RYAN

Katie Ryan, raised in Minnesota, eventually moved to California where she incorporated her love of horses to help others through equine therapy. She is a licensed Marriage and Family Therapist with a private practice in Valencia. Katie recently started a Military Equestrian Program called Synergy along with four of her colleagues. This program helps veterans to heal wounds of war and family relationships by using horses as part of the treatment team.

A horse related ankle injury led her to a new interest - writing. Katie has already written one book, *Horse Wisdom Alchemy*, which was published in January of 2014. She also published an article about Don Edwards the cowboy singer in *Range Magazine* in 2015. Katie's second book, *Blood Moon*, a mystery, will be out in early 2016.

Currently she is writing and producing a documentary called *Coyote* about the cowboy singer Don Edwards; it is due out in 2016. She is proud to be part of the Antelope Valley Writers Association and their anthologies and appreciates the feedback and friendships.

BLOOD MOON (An Excerpt)

(The following is an excerpt from Chapter One of Katie Ryan's book in progress entitled, *Blood Moon*.)

How beautiful is night!
A dewy freshness fills the silent air;
No mist obscures; nor cloud, nor speck, nor stain,
Breaks the serene of heaven:
In full orbed glory, yonder moon divine
Rolls through the dark blue depths;
Beneath her steady ray
The desert circle spreads
Like the round ocean, girdled with the sky.
How beautiful is night!

by Robert Southey (1744-1843)

The stars are shining brightly on the no-street-light town of Deep Valley. The couple in the red cabin along the main street was sleeping soundly. Suddenly Daniel was awakened to the sound of thundering hooves. Was he dreaming? He had recently watched an episode on TV where horses were the only transportation, so maybe his subconscious had latched on to that notion.

Daniel rolled over to try to re-settle. At that moment his wife Cari was also struggling to stay asleep. She heard it too - the sound of hooves on the pavement. She slipped out of bed to go take a look as Daniel joined her at the window.

Sure enough their eyes and ears were not mistaken. There were three horses in the dark running in circles just down the street from their humble abode. The moonlight caught the shape and strength of their legs and carriages. One horse in particular was enormous - perhaps a Percheron or Belgian mix?

Daniel had been brought up with horses; in fact, his mother was a horse trainer preparing young horses to become race horses for the track. He knew too well that once a horse is spooked they will run from their real or imagined danger.

Even though Daniel was irritated about being awakened in the middle of the night, he knew he needed to take action or the horses could be hit by early morning rush hour traffic. An older mare was killed on the road a year earlier, a sad ending to her long life.

He pulled on his jeans as his wife put on her robe. He went outside to see if he could find a rope or something that resembled a halter, even though he knew only his mother had halters of all shapes and sizes a few miles away.

As he went outside to grab even a shoestring, he noticed all three horses were heading north up the canyon road which spelled danger for the commuters that race down the canyon from ten miles away. He quickly yelled at Cari to call Animal Control. Couldn't they bring a trailer and know how to corral the runaway bandits? Daniel jumped into his jeep and headed towards the merry threesome as they ran up the road. When they heard the jeep the larger one slowed down and moved to the left out of the middle of the road. Daniel pulled over wondering how he could possibly wrangle this large equine with only a broken rope attached to a shoestring.

Just as he got out of the jeep he hoped and prayed no late night bar hoppers would come flying down the hill. After all it was a full moon which brought out the crazies. The big horse turned around as he approached, and he could see the whites of its eyes telling him this wasn't going to be easy. The other two horses, which to the best he could figure, were both bay horses. One was fairly tall and the other much smaller and more compact. The smaller one lifted his tail much like you'd see an Arabian horse do as it pranced in circles.

Daniel approached the big one cautiously from the side and attempted to put the makeshift rope around its large neck. He figured it to be a mare that swiftly swung her neck, and the force nearly knocked him to his knees. She ran straight west up an embankment. The other two horses followed. By this time Daniel knew he would need reinforcements because it would take a miracle to lasso these runaway trains by himself in the dark, with no halter or lead rope. It brought to mind an old movie he had seen called *The Misfits* where a group of folks including Marilyn Monroe and the *Gone with the Wind* star (what was his name again?) were hired to capture wild horses by truck, plane, and other cruel measures. Daniel pretty much knew these were not wild horses because the big one looked really well fed. They were merely on a joy ride hoping to be home by feeding time.

Since they were now off the main road up the embankment, Daniel decided he would head back home to see if his wife had any luck with Animal Control. As Daniel pulled into the driveway, Cari met him with, "Animal Control is on its way."

"What a relief maybe I can go back to bed after this is all over. It's now 3 a.m. so I may even call Mom to see if she can help."

"I already called the Sheriff's Office and they informed me they would come check it out - when they could." Living in an unincorporated area did not give them priority. "You'd think after the last horse getting hit they'd come but he wasn't hopeful."

Daniel started pillaging through his small garage that was in bad need of cleaning up. It had only been four months since they had moved into their cabin and still the unpacking wasn't complete. The birds were not even awake as he came across a long strap used to tie down cargo in the back of a truck bed. Meanwhile his wife was on the computer to put out an alert to anyone in the area who might be missing horses.

He grabbed the strap, put on his hiking boots, and grabbed a frozen waffle back in the house. He didn't want to lose track of the three amigos. He jumped in his jeep just as Animal Control was pulling up. There was no horse trailer in sight; only the regular dogcatcher vehicle. Didn't his wife tell them these were horses? The sleepy driver was missing two teeth as he sauntered over to the jeep. Daniel asked, "Where is the horse trailer?"

The man yawned and replied, "We'll have to do an investigation before we can authorize a trailer. Sorry, company policy." Daniel didn't have time for long explanations so he motioned for the dog catcher to follow him.

Daniel wondered what the heck the guy was going to do with his dogcatcher vehicle, but he figured two bodies to maneuver that big mare were better than one. He pulled his jeep over at the gravel turnout next to a ranch that also had horses in their arena. If only he could get them over to that arena at least they would be safe. The ranch horses were pacing back and forth whinnying to the threesome on the hill. Daniel jumped out with his cargo strap as the toothless dogcatcher pulled up. The dogcatcher grabbed a long metal pole with a hook on the end.

Daniel thought, *Yeah, the horses will really appreciate that. They will spook to the next county.* He just shook his head and the dogcatcher got the message and left it in the truck. It occurred to Daniel that this Animal Control guy knew absolutely nothing about how to handle animals.

Daniel and his worthless partner walked across the road to the embankment and saw the horses had scurried up near the Forest Service cabin. All three heads jerked up and he noticed a red hue reflected on their muscular bodies. That's right, it was the full red blood moon. He had considered getting up tonight to check it out but quickly dismissed it, wanting sleep instead. Now he was seeing it by default, having been catapulted out of bed by these riders in the sky, and had a front row seat to the red moon. Too bad he had to share it with the toothless wonder. Why does someone lose their front teeth? Meth? Lack of brushing? He didn't have time to ponder these questions now.

Daniel slowly approached the big blonde mare as he said, "Easy now easy girl." Boy was she big. The little bay put his tail in the air and started snorting and prancing; the other bigger bay close behind nipped at the small bay's withers. As he observed these two, Daniel moved to the side of the big girl and quickly threw the strap around her neck. She started to bolt and realized she'd been had.

Daniel grabbed the strap and moved the large horse down the embankment. As he inched her down, her large dinner plate hooves caught on something in a small ravine. Daniel continued to pull on the strap and realized her hoof was actually caught on something. As he got closer he caught the sight of the red full moon again, glowing directly above with a strange foggy calmness. He said, "Easy girl we'll get you lose." He looked down and noticed a grey-blue tarp with a tear where her foot was caught.

The dogcatcher was just making his way up the embankment as Daniel moved towards the hock of the great Palomino and gave it a tap which caused her to lift her leg. *I would not want to be her farrier but at least she knows how to lift her leg on cue*, Daniel thought. As he was clearing the tarp and torn strands for her hoof he saw the arm protruding from under the tarp. The horses seemed to become suddenly aware of the increase in blood pressure to Daniels startled face. The two bays scampered up further and the Palomino showed the whites of her eyes once more and snorted loudly.

Daniel raised his hand towards the dogcatcher as if to warn him to stay back. Not only was Daniel dealing with three spooked horses, but now he had come across something that could change going back to bed anytime soon. While holding the Palomino he yelled to the dogcatcher, "Go back to my cabin and call the Sheriff; tell him there is a body up here." *Now they will need to find some time in their schedules to come pronto*, he thought. "I will bring the horses down from the hill and meet you at the cabin."

The dogcatcher started to say, "Whaaat!?" but saw the look on Daniel's face and headed for his rig.

BEFORE COWBOY MUSIC

Before Cowboy Music and the balladeers
who tell their stories so clear

I could only imagine anything so dear

One night in our fancy cowboy attire in William S Hart's home

I understood the poet and musician's need to roam

The wide open space of a Texas plain

Could cure the wandering soul's pain

The red rocks of the Southwest in all its mystical grandeur

Explains humanity's need to take a tour

When Don Edwards sang "When the work's all done this fall"
and "Ramblin' Cowboy"

I was transported to an era I wished I had known

From Little Joe the Wrangler to the Strawberry Roan

Now that I was on this trail of the Milky Way and my favorite
horse

I knew I couldn't come back from its magic and ever be alone

I will follow the path of the drovers and the freedom to sing

I will stop and appreciate nature and the bird on the wing

Perhaps one day the people will also take heed

To slow down and connect to animals and the land

To learn from the cowboy singers to take their lead

For now I'll listen carefully to their stories of the West

And carry the message of the coyote's wail

To my friends and neighbors to heed this quest

FLORIDA JOHNS

Florida "Flo" Johns is a retired administrative assistant who has a great appreciation for family, friends and all things of natural beauty.

She attended Mississippi Valley State University, majoring in Business Administration. More recently, she has completed Information Technology courses at West Los Angeles College. Ms. Johns relocated to Los Angeles in the late 1960s, and now resides in the Antelope Valley.

She finds great pleasure in interacting with people and tends to look for the best in everyone and make the best of every situation. She enjoys spending time with her adult children, grandchildren, and great-grandchild. Ms. Johns is currently writing her memoirs in hopes of eventually completing an autobiography.

THE THREE AIRMEN

The first airman is my brother who is two years my senior. Unfortunately, we did not grow up together. Even though we lived across town from each other, we had very little contact. My brother and I shared seven siblings, and all except four, each of us was either adopted or placed in the homes of other family members.

Upon high school graduation, my brother attended college for one year but after one too many conflicts in a chaotic home environment, he decided to drop out of college and enlist in the United States Air Force.

After completing basic training at Lackland AFB in San Antonio, Texas, he was assigned to a newly formed on the job training program, and was trained as a communications specialist serving in Asia and Southeast Asia for more than four years.

Upon receiving an honorable discharge, he settled down in the Los Angeles area and reconnected with our mother. He used his experiences and those skills learned in the USAF to secure employment in the aircraft industry where he remained for many years.

As an adult, I was able to reunite with my brother in the late 1960s, and although not as close as we should be, he is the one person I can always rely on to give me sound advice. He has a logical and level headed approach to most situations.

In the late 1970s, our mother passed away and soon afterward, my brother moved to the Las Vegas area where he pursued various business ventures. After several business attempts, he returned to Los Angeles and was able to gain employment with the USPS. He remained there until his recent retirement. Now happily married, he continues to reside in the Los Angeles area.

My high school boyfriend also enlisted in the USAF soon after high school graduation. Like my brother, he also completed basic training at Lackland AFB. He was stationed at Eglin AFB in Pensacola, Florida, where he was assigned to a ground transport service unit. One of the first things he did while at Eglin was to purchase a 1965 metallic gray Mustang. It was so nice and has always been my dream car. Unfortunately, things did not work out for us and we went our separate ways. I often wonder what would have happened if I had remained in that relationship.

Some years later, we reconnected and would see each other from time to time as he became a long distance truck driver, driving from the east coast to the west coast and back. My friend would always make contact with me if he came anywhere near Los Angeles.

Over the years, we lost contact with each other but I will always have fond memories of him because, every now and then, I come across a sweater he gave me for Christmas when I was sixteen years old. It still looks pretty good.

The third airman is my son. Basically, my son was not a behavioral problem as a teenager; however, I was concerned about his safety just the same. You see, we lived in a drug-ridden, gang-infested neighborhood. Although not the worst, it was far from being the best. Having been married and divorced twice, I was a single mother of three doing the best I could to keep my children safe and from becoming a part of their environment.

My son was a good student. He had a part-time job at McDonalds all through high school, and participated in a mentoring program sponsored by a well known life insurance company.

Additionally, he received a partial scholarship for participating in the program. However, in his spare time, he liked to party with his friends and go to teen dance clubs in the Hollywood area.

Prior to his high school graduation my son expressed a desire to attend college, which was a good thing; however, I had reservations as to his overall commitment in pursuing this endeavor. He was still working at McDonalds. It was peacetime, and I suggested that he enlist in the armed services and, to the best of my ability, explained to him some of the benefits of doing so. There were military recruiters readily available on his high school campus, and I was visited in my home by at least two of them. Ultimately, we decided he should enlist in the United States Air Force.

Within a few weeks after graduating, he was on his way to Lackland AFB for basic training. Upon finishing basic training, he was stationed at Edwards AFB. A year or so later, he was transferred to Spangdahlem Air Base near Frankfurt, Germany. After serving at Spangdahlem for three years, he received an honorable discharge, returned to the United States, and settled down in the Antelope Valley. As an airman in the USAF, he received training in logistics in addition to earning some college credits. He has since used his experience and training to earn his MBA in addition to a Bachelor's Degree in Logistics.

My son is currently a contract specialist for the Department of Defense. I give credit to the discipline, experience, and training he received in the USAF for the success he enjoys today. He is happily married and resides in Palmdale, California.

It is admirable that these three airmen were able to employ the discipline, experiences, skills, and training acquired in the United States Air Force to secure long-term competitive employment positions; make adequate adjustments to civilian life; and achieve some measure of success.

PRETTY LADY

Hey, pretty lady you're so fine

To gaze upon your face is divine

Hey, pretty lady who are you

Looking so beautiful with your new hairdo

Hey, pretty lady you're dressed to kill

Stepping out in your shiny high heels

Hey, pretty lady where did you go

Please come again, your little girl misses you so.

A WEEKEND IN PARIS

In the summer of 1992, my son, who was in the United States Air Force and stationed at Spangdahlem Air Base outside of Frankfurt, asked me if I would like to visit him and his wife in Germany as he had decided not to re-enlist and would be coming home by the end of the year. They were planning to spend the 4th of July weekend in Paris. Even though money was tight, I decided that I would travel to Germany and join them on their trip to Paris.

Before my travel arrangements could be made, my youngest daughter, who was fifteen at the time, decided she would like to accompany me. As I had planned to stay only one week and barely had enough money for my trip, let alone airfare for her, we decided to contact her father, and he agreed to help with her airfare. I agreed with this arrangement with the exception that our daughter would not be returning with me within a week but would stay in Germany for an additional six weeks.

The next step was to obtain our passports as we both had only ever traveled from Los Angeles to New Orleans and back. I first went to the local post office and was referred to another location only to learn that the passport applications were only taken on certain days and times.

With all the running around here and there, we decided to go to the Federal Building in Westwood to apply for our passports. When we arrived, there was a room full of people, many of whom were sitting, leaning against walls, or standing in lines. I thought, *this is going to take all day.* However, after standing in line a short while and finally making it to the window, our several previous trips paid off. Our paperwork was in order; things went smoothly and we were done quickly.

We spent the next few weeks going through our closets trying to decide what clothes we would take on our trip. We purchased a few items to add to our favorites and began to pack.

During the time leading up to our travel date, I was making myself sick worrying about how I would occupy my time during such a long flight. Once our travel date arrived and we boarded the plane, I had calmed down a bit. Our flight was made more comfortable by the flight attendants serving a variety of munchies such as sweet breads and cookies. The flight attendants also provided us with warm herb-soaked towels to freshen up, which added to our comfort. There were movies to watch, and I kept my headphones on all the while listening to songs like "Danny Boy," "Rain Drops Keep Falling on My Head," and "You are My Sunshine." I even managed to fall asleep from time to time, never taking my headphones off.

Finally, we arrived in Frankfurt somewhere around noon the next day. We were met at the airport by my son and his wife. My son took us to their two bedroom apartment located in a little village just a short distance from Spangdahlem. After showing us our bedroom which contained a freestanding bathroom sink and thin metal pull-down shutters at the windows, I pulled down the shutters and got into bed for a quick nap, as we had to be at Spangdahlem by 4:00 p.m. to board a bus for our trip to Paris.

After awaking from my nap and freshening up a bit, we hurried to the base where we boarded a bus and traveled to a large sparsely lit parking lot where there were dozens of buses headed to different European locations. After going through rows of buses, we finally found one that read PARIS, and we boarded. On the bus, we met our tour guide who told us that she worked at the bank on base and spoke three languages: German, French and English.

We all thought we were surely on our way to Paris by now but were mistaken. Although most of the seats on the bus were already taken, we still made stops at two more military installations, Ramstein and Mannheim, where we picked up a few more servicemen. Finally, we were on our way to Paris.

After an all-night bus ride with a few stops in between, we arrived in Paris early Saturday morning. The first thing we did was go to breakfast in a coffee shop. The breakfast offerings at this shop were few, consisting only of baguettes, croissants, apples, oranges, coffee, tea, or juice. I distinctly remember my son pulling out what he called the "equalizer" (deli ham and smoked turkey slices).

In the meantime, our tour guide had set up shop at one of the tables where she sold tickets to places that were not included in our tour packets. We purchased the Seine River boat tour.

After breakfast, the first place we visited was the Louvre. Our tour guide did not accompany the group to the exhibits, but we were told what time to be back at the bus. The one exhibit I really wanted to see was the Mona Lisa. We found that exhibit only to find a large crowd of tourists like ourselves lingering in front of it. However, we at some point were able to get close enough to get a glimpse of the masterpiece. It was set inside the wall of the museum behind a glass window with instructions to the effect that the use of flashbulbs were prohibited as it causes a deterioration of the painting. This being the pre-smartphone era, we were just out of luck. Next, we visited the Venus de Milo exhibit and a few others, but these were the ones that stood out in my mind.

Then it was back on the bus and off to visit the Eiffel Tower which, explained to us by our tour guide, had been erected as an entry way to the World's Fair held in Paris in the 1800s. To our disappointment, we were not allowed to enter as there were too many people in our group, and it would take too long for us to tour the tower. Our tour guide further explained that as the tower got smaller some people would have to get off the elevator; therefore, it would take too long for all of us to reach the top. So we lingered around the base of the tower, took pictures with our disposable cameras, and bought cold treats from nearby vendors.

After boarding the bus at the Eiffel Tower, we continued on our city tour. Our tour guide pointed out the Military School of Napoleon Bonaparte and the Arc de Triomphe, which is a memorial to fallen French soldiers. He added that it also held the Tomb of the Unknown Soldier.

The roundabout was a bit confusing and made me wonder how we would enter into traffic safely. We did, and continued on our way; however, we did have a minor traffic accident as the bus driver tried to ease the bus down a narrow street lined with small cars parked halfway on the sidewalk and halfway in the street. At one point, the bus became entangled with the back bumper of a small car. Several airmen, who were seated near the front of the bus, got off to see what had happened. They determined that no damage was done, and the airmen lifted up the small car and placed it farther onto the sidewalk. After everyone returned to their seats, the bus driver was able to drive through the narrow street without further incident. Our tour guide explained to us that if there had been damage to the other car, the owner would be responsible for any repairs due to France's no-fault insurance policy.

We were now on our way to check in at the Holiday Inn-Marseilles. Later that evening we returned to Paris for dinner. On the way, our tour guide pointed out the University of Sorbonne, the Opera House, and the Moulin Rouge. Not everyone in our group was going to dinner with us. Some were going to the Moulin Rouge, where LaToya Jackson was the featured artist with a ridiculous cover charge, and others were going elsewhere. As we got off the bus, the tour guide told us that we had to be back to this location by midnight or we would have to get our own transportation back to the hotel.

With that said, the majority of the group went to a nearby tavern, up a narrow staircase to a dimly lit private dining room. There was one very long table and two smaller tables with place settings. At each setting there was a French roll with a tiny American flag on a toothpick protruding from the top, similar to that of a cocktail umbrella. The dinner choices were baked salmon or beef medallions, with roasted vegetables and iced tea. There were also two small slices of cheese on a separate plate that I did not like the taste of and passed on those. My dinner choice was the baked Salmon which was smothered in a delicious white sauce. For dessert, there was flaming baked Alaska, which I had heard of but had never seen or tasted. The presentation was exciting and it was so delicious. Additionally, as we ate dinner, the servers played songs on their accordions such as the "Star Spangled Banner," "Yankee Doodle," and "God Bless America." This made our evening truly a 4th of July celebration.

After dinner, we went onto the terrace of the tavern where we witnessed a breathtakingly beautiful skyline of Paris at night, with the Eiffel Tower standing tall as well as other monuments aglow with hundreds, if not thousands, of tiny dazzling golden lights. Then, as instructed, our group met at the prearranged location in time to return to our hotel.

Early the next morning, we arose early and gathered our things before breakfast as we would not be returning to the hotel. After having a breakfast consisting of croissants, fruit spreads, and orange juice, we were on our way to Paris for more sightseeing.

The first stop for the day was the Norte Dame Cathedral. Most of us did a walkthrough, and the ceiling and stained glass windows were sights to behold.

Next, we were allowed an hour for souvenir shopping. I bought Eiffel Tower key chains, paper weights, coasters, and other gifts for co-workers, but mostly for myself. Then we were off to Park des Etats-Unis where in the middle of the small park stood a replica of the Statue of Liberty. Our tour guide explained to us that our Statue of Liberty was a gift to the United States from the French government.

Afterwards, we took the riverboat tour of the Seine River. The tour guide was very knowledgeable, pointing out interesting sights on the riverbank. We even managed a quick stop at a perfume factory and a flea market.

The last stop on our weekend in Paris was the Palace of Versailles. The palace was a massive structure with beautifully landscaped gardens and fountains. I was in awe when walking down the palatial hall of mirrors with bigger than life mirrors, huge chandeliers, richly decorated walls and ceiling, and gold and crystal statuettes. Our tour guide explained the absence of furnishings in the palace due to pilfering during the French Revolution and that many pieces could still be found throughout the world. After visiting the gift shop, we were ready to board the bus and return to Germany.

This was the end of my weekend in Paris, and it was a very exciting and enjoyable one. The trip allowed me to go places and witness things I had only read about in books or seen in movies. I collected quite a few souvenirs and made a scrapbook of my travels, which I used to refresh my memory while writing this story.

ESPERANZA BELTRÁN

Esperanza Beltrán is currently a stay at home. She has three children - two still at home and one who has recently left the nest to attend college. She has always enjoyed writing but has only recently begun to take it seriously, writing stories about her family and heritage. She is currently working on her first book which is based her grandmother's life, growing up in Oaxaca, Mexico.

Besides writing, Esperanza also enjoys drawing and painting which she tries to practice often. Above all, she has always been an avid reader. Some of her favorite books are *Like Water for Chocolate, The House on Mango Street, Angela's Ashes,* and *Buddha in the Attic.*

HER HOUSE

The house is small and off-white; the steps are stone. The door is of wood and when you open it everything explodes. The walls are a *rosa mexicano*; the ceiling a is sunshine color. The chairs have plain old standing up and lying down lines. They're made by the hands of the *viejito* who lives down the street, who walks with one foot and jumps with the other. The floor is roughed up, covered in rugs the size of comfort; they're wool and hand-woven with bright colors that hurt your eyes if you look at them for too long.

There are no machines, except for an old stereo set on the only station that works, the one that plays Lila Downs, Violeta Parra, Lola Beltrán and Antonio Aguilar all day long. *"El tiempo pasaaaa y no te puedo olvidaaaaar"* bursts out of the stereo's circular speakers. From the corner of the room a clack, clack, clack chorus accompanies it. Clack. Clack. Clack-clack-clack-clack-clack-clack. Metal against paper, one letter after another and another, fast-fast-fast until papers begin to fly out into the air and sway left to right until they land flat on the floor. One after another and another until they cover the floor like a fresh cap of snow.

Disappearing slowly behind the noise sits a girl. She faces a window that looks out to a garden that echoes the colors of the room that surrounds her. Her eyes are closed; she wants to feel the colors shooting at her "like rays of sunshine," that's what the *gabachos* say.

But that's what she wants. To feel the colors, warm against her skin, penetrating so that she may carry them with her to the white emptiness in front of her. She wears no shoes and her toes curl up in excitement, clack-clack-clack-clack, a pencil in her hair, strands fall like *fiesta* streamers.

The words and sentences come like tiny fish in the waves that have risen above her somewhere, she doesn't quite know. Like a good *pescadora* she captures them, one by one, slowly, patiently.

And when she finishes, she sets her feet on the hand-woven wool rug, the red one with the little turquoise squares joined together until they become a diamond shape, and black and white borders that look like the waves that carried the words like fish above her head. She stretches her arms, her legs, her voice, until it reaches Lola's voice coming from the old round speakers, *Cucurucucuuú* . . .

Her lungs give in, her voice cracks but her feet continue moving forward, back, forward, back, forward, forward, forward, one arm hugs her stomach and the other is bent into the air. She dances her way into the kitchen; she's hungry.

The *mole* her mother made yesterday calls to her. The rice, the chicken, and the handmade *tortillas*. The smell of *chiles* and onion, garlic and cumin. If she had tried to make it herself . . . unrealistic. She's no cook; the kitchen is her broken limb. She uses it but cautiously; the water burns and the stove resists.

The kitchen is white, white walls and white cabinets. White, the cabinet doors that open to reveal another explosion of color. Birds appear in cups and flowers bloom inside bowls. It's okay, she understands, the kitchen is not for all. She takes her wooden spoon, a crutch, and begins. The mole steams in her *olla de barro* and the *pierna de pollo* awaits the encounter. They meet in the blooming flower and the bird floats alongside, holding water, holy water.

The cactus in the windowsill is finally thirsty. She prays to the cactus, please live, please don't die! Not you too! Holy water, sprinkle, sprinkle, live. But the cactus doesn't know, holy water, tap water, spring water, water water. She sips and she remains. She lives and has a baby. A flower, red like the hand-woven rug with turquoise diamond and black and white waves. The girl smiles, *mole* in her mouth, on her lips, her fingertips. On 'love' and 'heart' and 'roots', *mole* in her stomach, now she can keep going. Clack-clack-clack . . .

Cucurucucuuú palomaaaa . . .

RICHARD C. ELTON, M.D.

Dr. Richard Elton received his Medical Degree in 1956 and has been practicing orthopedic surgery for many years until he retired from private practice in 2000. To fill his free time he started writing and has enjoyed composing poems, short commentaries, and stories of his experiences. He married his wife, Joan, in 1953 and they have four children and a bunch of grand and great grand children whom they dearly love. Dr. Elton is also a retired U. S. Army Surgeon (1979, Colonel) and did tours in Vietnam (1967-68) where he was present during the Tet Offensive in Qui Nhon, and in Germany (1974-78) where he recollects the horror of the Berlin Wall that kept people from leaving East Germany and East Berlin, with its manned machine gun posts and spikes pointed inward not outward.

PRESSED PANTS

At the time, we were classmates at Newton High School, Massachusetts, in our junior year. I lived in Newton Highlands and he lived in Newton Lower Falls but I did not know his name. We were between classes when he came up to me and asked if I would mind if he asked a question. Certainly, I would not mind and I prompted him to proceed.

He hesitated just a bit then asked, "How do you keep your pants so neatly pressed every day?"

I thought about this briefly and the picture of my mother at the ironing table each morning came to mind, so I told him, "My mother presses them every morning before I come to school."

His head went up as he seemed to lower and close his eyes, and I could imagine him saying "of course" to himself, as the answer seemed to be so obvious (in 1947 clothes lost their press quickly).

I had never given my pressed pants a second thought until I learned this boy had noticed them with some envy, and then, of course, I felt badly to think this boy's mother probably chided him for his wrinkled pants but did not iron them frequently for him.

Thank goodness for today's technology and pants that do not lose their press.

HEAVEN

There is a place called Heaven, the path is hard to walk.
Love and Trust and Faith must Be, and not just Talk.

The path is strewn with stones, some big and many small;
We trip, we slip, we slide. Our balance lost, we fall.

We're bruised and hurt a bit but get back up and heal
We keep a'going on, the greater is our zeal.

We love and cherish all His throng, though we don't understand
Why some do the things they do, that do not seem so grand.

Our lot is not to judge. Pride will get in our way.
We live now in the dark of night, in Heaven we'll see the day.

The light of God will shine about. All things will be illum'd.
Our earthly clothing and desires, from us will be de-plumed.

GOOD DOG SPOT

Dog stories abound; here's mine.

We called him Spot. He was part Border Collie with long black and white hair and perhaps his legs were a little longer. He was beautiful. He was a little more than a puppy when we took him home from the animal shelter at Fort Hood, Texas. He seemed quite smart and I quickly taught him to stay and come. I built a nice big doghouse for him, which my two small boys went in and out of in their playing, but Spot simply dug a hole on each side and rested there.

I took walks with Spot around the block and taught him to heel, which he learned quickly and could soon be walked without a leash. He would also stay sitting on the back seat of my Volkswagen Beetle convertible, usually with the top down, while I would go into a store or into the side entrance of the hospital where I worked. Sometimes I was gone for up to thirty minutes in my office and Spot would stay right there on the back seat, never jumping out of the car.

He came with us on Boy Scout hikes. I was a Scout Leader at the time, and Spot came along with us to a Jamboree. The boys all loved him and he would mind his manners well. One day the Commanding Officer of Fort Hood came to review the scouts at the Jamboree. As he passed in his jeep, Spot was right there on the side of the road with all the other scouts lined up on each side. The general got a big kick out of that and gave Spot a big smile.

The only trouble we had with Spot was because of a next door neighbor's dog. I would let Spot go free at times because there was a big expanse behind our house where he could run and not bother anyone. He would chase rabbits.

One day I watched him chase one, each going as fast as the other, until the rabbit came to a cyclone fence encircling an electric facility of some sort. The rabbit jumped up as high as he could only to bump into the fence and fall to the ground as Spot came upon him. Spot then turned to look at me as if to ask, "What do I do now?" This was his first and only catch so far as I know. Spot picked up the rabbit and brought it home to the backyard and did what came naturally; he ate the rabbit then and there.

But one day the neighbor complained that I was not complying with the leash law. I wasn't at first, but even chained, Spot broke free several times to visit the pretty German Shepherd next door. Then one day the neighbor's dog got free and came into our backyard. I had the pleasure of escorting her back to where she belonged, and we had no further reports of "dog not on leash."

Then came the War and when Spot had been with us just one and one half years I had to go to Vietnam. We could not keep him. We gave him to an Army sergeant who was going to retire and live in the country on a farm. This would be an excellent place for Spot to live out his years. However, a few days later while I was at work in my office, a friend came to say there was a dog in the doorway of the hospital and it looked just like Spot.

And there he was, lying in the side doorway through which he'd seen me go in and out as he waited many times on the back seat of the Volkswagen. I took him back to the sergeant's house and never saw Spot again, but he will always have a place in my heart.

THE TET OFFENSIVE

I was stationed at the 85th U.S. Army Hospital outside the city of Qui Nhon, Vietnam on January 30, 1968, when the Tet Offensive began. Simultaneously some 80,000 North Vietnamese soldiers and Viet Cong troops attacked 100 towns and cities to try to turn the tide of war in their favor. Qui Nhon was one of the cities.

I remember the calling of a Red Alert that night. I was a colonel in the Medical Corps. Since my arrival in June 1967, I had been using all my orthopedic skills cleansing gunshot and fragment wounds of the extremities of our soldiers, and those of prisoner patients, both Viet Cong and North Vietnamese soldiers.

I was now approached by our defense forces, given an army rifle, and told to stand guard at the doorway to one of the wards of patients in a Quonset hut. I sat on the bed near the door and was fully aware that if the enemy should come through I was resolved to shoot them and thus protect the American soldier patients confined to their beds. Fortunately, this resolve never came to the test. I don't recall hearing gunfire in the distance though there may well have been some that night. We were all aware that something different was happening.

The night passed and the next day the Adjutant asked me if I would like to ride into Qui Nhon city in a jeep with him to see what had occurred there. He felt it was safe enough. There had been very little fighting in our area. So I went along with him, and saw firsthand the bodies of five or six Viet Cong men who had tried to take over a radio station but were shot and killed in the process. They were lying in a region that looked like a small park, with grass and some benches. The radio station was nearby up on the second floor of a building.

We drove back to the 85th Hospital without incident. Subsequent reports came in of uprisings, attacks actually with attempted but unsuccessful uprisings, for the most part in many different cities. The reader can refer to other sources for basic information on the Tet Offensive. For my part, we surgeons simply treated the soldiers as they were brought to us from Khe Sanh and other active fighting places.

The basic intent of wound surgery was to clean the wound of dirt and foreign debris, and to cautiously cut out dead tissue, being careful not to injure nearby arteries and nerves. We would leave the wounds open for two to five days, and then close the skin if the wound looked healthy and free of dead tissue. Most of these wounds would heal up very well and broken bones would be dealt with at a later date, if necessary.

My father joined the Cavalry just as WWI ended. Then he saw active duty as a doctor (Pathologist) during WWII. Vietnam was now "my war," and I felt I had been well trained to do my job. I was a professional, plying my profession, and did not get emotionally attached to my patients. The first and last casualties I saw, on entering and exiting the Country, were American soldiers who had stepped on land mines and had both their legs blown off. Such are the trials of war.

I never cried in Vietnam. I was simply doing a job that had to be done. But many years later when the Gulf War was launched in August of 1990, I did cry. I cried because I knew that young men were going to get hurt, some badly, and I felt sorry for them, unknown though they may be to me and fighting on either side. These young men had families who cared for them. Yes, I cried for them and do so still.

Wars have raged throughout history so it is doubtful they will ever stop. Yet, at my tender age of eighty-five, I do harbor hope they will stop, or at least produce fewer and fewer casualties. On the other hand, I can't help but think, if the atomic bomb continues to be "out there," I must conclude one will be set off sometime, somewhere. If so, heaven help us.

THE BERLIN WALL

The Berlin Wall was erected in 1961 by the German Democratic Republic which was the name given East Berlin by its Communist Russian possessor and ruler. The wall was built to keep people from leaving East Berlin and East Germany to enter West Berlin.

One day I saw that wall and noted that the spikes were pointing inward, not outward, and guard towers indeed set up a "Death Strip" presumably all along the perimeter of the wall. I tried to imagine not being able to cross a wall built by my own government and just the thought sent chills up my spine.

I was stationed in Frankfurt, Germany, from 1974 to 1978 and, as Orthopedic Consultant to the U. S. Army Europe, I made several trips into West Berlin to visit the Army Hospital there. On one such occasion I made a trip into East Berlin at Checkpoint Charlie. I had a proper Army escort. I recall seeing the very drab mass housing buildings for many of the people. These were simply large rectangular buildings, painted a single color, with little or no shrubbery or lawn, sort of out in the middle of nowhere, and I could imagine many similar rooms in them.

We were able to window shop at several stores, and in one store I found a table piece, a wood carved Christmas carousel powered by the heat of a ring of candles at the bottom, and by a horizontal propeller at the top. This interested me and I wanted to buy it. The price was $80.00. However, the U.S. Army had come up with a rule that only $50.00 worth of merchandise could be brought back into West Berlin.

This was, I was told, because things were cheaper in East Berlin, and army personnel in the know would buy cheap in East Berlin and then sell at a profit in West Berlin. Apparently this practice had to stop. So I brought up this problem and was immediately assured there was no problem. I would simply be given a receipt for $50.00 to show to the guard at Checkpoint Charlie. I paid the $80.00 and reflected that capitalism would always find a way to do business no matter the rules.

During my years in Germany I had two other reflections of life behind The Iron Curtain. My secretary at the U. S. Army Hospital, Frankfurt, had a sister in East Germany. She told me she could write letters but had to be very careful of what she wrote because the letters were opened, read and censored by the government. The sisters rarely saw each other. Thus, I knew a person who was directly affected by the Cold War.

The other was a taxi driver who was taking me to the railroad station. He was quite talkative and told me of his family in Russia where he was born and raised. His father had owned a farm. The government offered to take it as communal property but he could still work it. Or, he could keep the farm in his name but then would have to pay taxes. He chose the latter. Then as time went by the taxes were raised until they got to the point the father could no longer support his family, so he capitulated and the farm became communal property. The taxi driver did choose to leave the country but his brother was still living in Russia. They, too, could not correspond freely.

I was happy to hear of the falling of the Berlin Wall in 1989 and the implosion of the communist government. People cannot be tied up forever. They must be allowed to each explore their own world in as free a manner as possible. I would like to think the world is getting to be a better place, over the few thousand years of recorded history, and I choose to remain optimistic in this regard.

God Bless The World.

JOAN MCCURDY ELTON

Joan Elton is the wife of Dr. Richard Elton, also a writer. She was born in Maine and spent her summers there. She and her family lived in Massachusetts the rest of the year. Joan graduated with a BS in Biology from Bates College, Lewiston, Maine and an MS in Education from the University of Massachusetts.

She met her husband after graduation when she worked at Amherst College as a research assistant. They were married in 1953 and she taught elementary school while he completed medical school and residency. When they began to adopt their family Joan stopped teaching and became an Army wife and mother. The family moved to the Antelope Valley in 1979 after Dr. Elton retired from twenty-three years as an Army orthopaedic surgeon. Joan became his office manager until their retirement in 2000. They share four children, nine grandchildren, and seven great-grandchildren. Joan is active in the Assistance League of Antelope Valley and in her church. She enjoys reading, writing, knitting, and being with her family.

DROUGHT 2015

My California lawn is parched and brown
Where once it wore a greener gown.

Water escapes our swimming pool.
We need the water to keep us cool.

Flowers don't like the thirst and heat.
They dry up and wilt without wet feet.

The ravens miss the sprinkler run-off.
They screech in anger and cawff and cawff.

Needles drift down from pines on high.
They fill up the gutters beneath a torrid sky.

We can complain that it's too darn hot
But until El Nino returns, it's all we've got.

58

MEMORIES OF MAINE

As a small child, many years ago, I lived in Massachusetts but spent my summers in Maine. My mother's parents owned a lake-front cottage on six lots of land on Sebago Lake in the southern part of the state. The lake was 9 by 12 miles and spring fed with a sandy bottom, a small beach for sand castles, a rock ledge for sunbathing and rocks to dive from when the lake was high. My mother, my sister, Betty, who was five years younger, and I would go there for the entire summer. Dad would join us the last two weeks before Labor Day. Grandma and Grandpa were there too, although Grandpa worked in Westbrook and arrived for dinner and on weekends with vegetables and zinnias from his home garden.

In the early years before electricity came to our part of the lake, we relied on kerosene lamps and a wood-burning stove. Water was pumped from the crystal-clear lake, so pure that a portion of it was a reservoir for the city of Portland. We had a two-holer beside the garage and thunder jugs under the beds.

The cottage originally had a screened-in porch on two sides. Early in my life this was converted to a front room with windows looking out on the lake, a bedroom for Mom and Dad, and a screened-in porch on the back corner. The front room had a fireplace and since my grandfather did some hunting, a deer's head with antlers hung over the fireplace and a black bearskin rug was in front of the hearth complete with head. I remember sitting on that head and counting his teeth. Upstairs were two more bedrooms with exposed wooden eaves. During obligatory nap time I imagined various animals and figures based on the shape of the knotholes. The cottage was furnished with castoffs from the city home. I loved the big brass beds and the quilts my grandmother and great-grandmother had made.

When the weather was good we played out-of-doors, swam, made sand castles, created houses from large appliance boxes our grandfather brought from the city, and traced pathways of sand and pebbles among the wildflowers in the woods. When the weather was inclement we played checkers and Go Fish, colored, and put together puzzles on a card table.

This was when my grandmother taught me to knit, and I sewed together knitted strips of colored wool for chair seat covers for the dining room. I worked with steel needles and always hated to put my work away when a thunderstorm was brewing.

Oh yes, we had chores, even when we were very little. We made our beds and picked up our room, dusted, swept the porch and the walk. I remember helping Grandma put coffee grounds and tea leaves on the roses. I don't remember the purpose, nourishment or to keep the bugs away, but it worked and the roses were beautiful as were all the perennials that grew around the cottage.

Dad did come to the lake one other time in the summer. That was Fourth of July weekend. Every evening, Gramps, Dad, and I got in the wooden rowboat with the outboard motor. We would head for Camel's Pasture, a strange hump in the lake which was unusually shallow and was great for catching smelts by hand line. Traveling out there and home we would troll for landlocked salmon. Also on the 4th, Dad would stage a cookout (we didn't know about BBQs). It was hamburgers and hotdogs, potato salad, and corn from the local farmer. Dad would float the corn, husks and all, in the lake until it was saturated and then place it on a grill on a rock wall and steam it over burning wood until it was black. To eat it we would pull back the husks and slather the kernels with butter. If it dripped it didn't matter because we were in our bathing suits. When it got dark Dad was in charge of the fireworks which he shot from the sunbathing ledge over the lake. This happened at all the other cottages. What a spectacle, and we always enjoyed the sparklers.

As we got older my sister and I went to camp for eight of those summer weeks. My grandparents died, and before long we were off to college. My dad died unexpectedly before my sister's senior year in college and soon we both were married. My mother returned to teaching after the death of my father, and since no one could be at the cottage with her during the summer, she chose to sell it. Afterwards, during vacations, she traveled or visited us. We were sorry to give up our summer home but we will always have those memories.

FRENETIC FEEDING OF FANTASTIC FINCHES

One spring, while visiting our son and his family in Virginia, we were introduced to a family of goldfinches eating birdseed from a net bag atop a pole in the backyard. The birds were fascinating to watch as they pulled the tiny black seeds through the netting and clung to the bag sideways, right-side up, and upside down. When we returned home to California I said, "I've got to have that!"

We obtained a long and narrow bird feeder of fine mesh wire, filled it with nyjer seed and hung it on a low branch of a tree in the backyard. Since that time, in season, the birds have flocked to the feeder and we've enjoyed watching their antics as they pull seeds through the wire, perching in dizzying acrobatic angles and arguing about who got there first.

This year we had some seed to begin the season, but when I attempted to buy a supply at the supermarket where I usually shop, there was none. Off to the pet store I went and they were all out until the weekend. Sunday we were back from the store and filled the feeder, using the table in a shaded alcove on the patio. For convenience I left the seed bags on the table.

It was not long before the flock discovered the newly filled feeder. Two days later I went out to fill the empty feeder only to be surprised by a small flock of finches flying up from their feast on the patio table. Apparently the service at our backyard was too slow and the birds were too smart.

MARY DENNING

Mary Denning has resided in the Antelope Valley for the past twelve years and in Southern California for most of her life. She and her husband Joe have raised six children. Mary is a graduate of California State University, Northridge, with a BA in Art. Her artwork has been exhibited and sold at galleries in San Fernando, Cambria, and Santa Cruz. One of her Mission paintings is part of the permanent collection of the San Fernando Mission.

Mary began writing after retiring from her job with the Los Angeles Library System. She enjoys composing short stories and poetry, and in recent years has won recognition in a local newspaper for one of her poems. Another poem recognized by the City of Palmdale won their inaugural "Walk on Words" contest. Mary's winning poem, "What Beauty Holds Us Captive Here," is preserved in cement in the Palmdale city square.

Recently she combined her knack for storytelling with her vibrant watercolors to write and illustrate her first children's book, "A Sunflower Story." Published in 2014, it is available on Amazon.com.

LETTERS

Up in the attic and under much dust

Lays a box filled with memories of just

Letters from loved ones received long ago

Tales of their daily lives we wanted to know

Linking the distance with words we compose

The first letter I ever wrote was to my good friend, Mr. Finney. The year was 1942. I was eleven. He had been my good friend and neighbor for the past three years. My family had moved to California that year, a long way from Ohio. Mr. Finney was missed, so I did the only thing I could to keep Mr. Finney close, I wrote to him.

We had moved next to the Finneys in 1939. Back then Acklin Avenue was a quiet shady street with modest homes and well-kept lawns. Most everybody had a front porch with a porch swing that was often occupied by whole families on a summer night because in those days no one had air-conditioning. Summer evenings in Ohio and close to Lake Erie were pretty hot and humid. Mosquitoes liked living there, too.

I introduced myself to Mr. Finney the first time I saw him. He appeared to be happy to make my acquaintance. We got off to a good start right away. Mr. Finney was an interesting guy. He owned a short wave radio and invited me into his home to enjoy listening to stations from all over the world. I was so impressed that we could sit in the Finney's living room and listen to people talking thousands of miles away. He had interesting rugs that hung on the walls - beautiful, richly colored Persian rugs that were hand woven. Each rug was like a book and told a story.

I was always impressed with Mr. Finney. He told me about a time when he was my age; he had experienced the great Chicago fire and told me all about it. How he saw people escaping from the fires in little boats across the Chicago River. Mr. Finney lived across the river where he was safe, but he said he stood on the shore and helped people to come ashore. From where he stood he said it looked like all of Chicago was on fire. The year was 1871 and the story of how that great fire started blamed it all on Mrs. O'Leary's cow that kicked over the barn lantern. Years later I discovered that a reporter made up that whole story.

I said "Wow" a lot when Mr. Finney told me stories about his life. Mrs. Finney and Mr. Finney moved into their house when they got married. He said they had a son, who died when he was a small child. He said his son would have been forty then. I thought at the time how sad for Mr. and Mrs. Finney. Even though at that time he was in his early eighties, Mr. Finney went off to work each morning in his three piece suit, always looking so distinguished. I was very proud to have a friend like Mr. Finney. He dealt in stocks and bonds, and that's all I ever knew about his work.

On all special occasions I received a book from the Finneys. Mr. Finney said he read each one first to be sure nothing improper would be found on its pages. Birthdays and Christmas and even Valentine's Day he would present me with a new book.

On many summer nights I was invited over to listen on his radio to *Fibber McGee and Molly* and *The Great Gildersleeve*. We thought those programs were hilarious. We were the best of friends, me and Mr. Finney.

And so I wrote a lot to Mr. Finney, told him how much I missed him and how I missed our interesting talks together, and sitting out in his backyard watching him use a slingshot to scare the squirrels off his prize cherry trees. And on hot summer nights, how I enjoyed counting all the stars in the skies with him.

I told him, too, about the Hollywood stars I had met. The bench where I caught the school bus was directly across the street from MGM studios. I could walk across and ask for stars' autographs. In those days, before the paparazzi, stars were more relaxed and friendly. Once when I was waiting for the bus and knitting khaki colored gloves for the Red Cross, (because World War II was on and everyone did something to help the soldiers), Gene Kelly came across the street and asked me what I was knitting. I explained that I was knitting for Britain. He said that was great and told me he had a little daughter. I saw Red Skelton often coming out of MGM's driveway; he always smiled and waved at us kids. I mailed all my autographs home to my play pals in Ohio. I never heard back from them, but Mr. Finney always wrote back.

One day I received a letter from Mrs. Finney. She said she was so sorry to inform me that my good friend Mr. Finney had died, and that she too would miss our evenings together sharing a root beer and listening to *Fibber McGee and Molly*. That was the only time I ever remembered my Mother telling me to stay home from school that day. She knew how much Mr. Finney meant to me.

Letters, memories so precious, are forever held in our hearts. Never to be forgotten.

AN UPHILL JOURNEY

Early morning darkness covered our city thus

And great gales of wind stirred up a mighty fuss

Courage was needed to be out in this strong gust

Driving up a hill surprised by what we trust

A little white crowned sparrow flying as he must

The mighty wind would push him down

But bold he would with courage frown

He'd readjust and carry on

When stormy winds would toss him round

Little sparrow would push head down

 The blackened rains were fierce and strong

Extinguishing his tired song

And everything was going wrong

His journey's destination was a bending hilltop tree

Where his safety and protection would bring him home free

 Determination was his creed

Amazed we watched this gallant breed

At last we heard him cry

"Oh Hell! This isn't wise"

Flying up against these mean skies

Could very well be my demise?

Grounded now he shouts "I'll improvise"

"I'll walk the damn hill before sunrise!"

OCTOBER

Softly she blows across the lands
And lovingly she waves her hands
To color all the Meadowlands

Her pallets colors, warm and gold
Richly adorned all to behold
For beauty such as hers delights
All the little Suburbanites

And children know it soon will be
Fun Trick or Treat festivities
Can't we all remember that glee?
Those years ago when we were three
And first we saw those painted trees

Where breezes danced within the leaves
Above the sounds where children sing
Remembered treats that smiles bring
And pumpkins set in rows like kings
October's beauty all aglow
Remembered thoughts from long ago

THOSE CRAZY HOLIDAYS

Thanksgiving was a joy
Gram's turkey came from Illinois
Uncle Robert brought all the boys
Aunt Naomi contained their noise
Cousin Ben forgot the McCoy's
All the McCoy's were quite annoyed
Blessings said and cooking enjoyed
When all were eating not a sound
Cause all enjoyed cuisine they found
When dishes done and kitchen cleaned
And Grandpa had naps in between
Everyone went home very pleased
Then Grandma took her apron off
Relaxed into a chair that's soft
Grandpa woke and announced with ease
"That went well, dinner was a breeze"
And Grandma smiled and did agree

A LETTER TO SANTA

Dear Santa, Has it been a busy year?
With so much to do it's a lot of wear
Do you get to rest sometimes in your chair?
Are your little elves helping with your care?
And are you still glad you chose that career?

I know the world over is glad you did
Cause Christmas magic comes for little kids
Sleeping in their beds dream of Santa's sled
Did you hear from Sebastian in Madrid?
Heard he asked for a tall gold pyramid.

How's Rudolph doing with that nose so cold?
Hope he's taking good care as he's been told
I've laid out hot chocolate and some snacks
You'll find them in the kitchen by the plaques.

Give my love to all, Dasher and Dancer
Prancer and Vixen, Comet and Donner,
Cupid and Blitzen and jolly old Rudolph
Bundle up Santa take care of your cough
Merry Christmas and a jolly sendoff.

REQUIEM FOR NORA

She had a lot of personality
A spunky little girl when only three
And capturing our hearts she made us see
That humor in most everything is free

One night when everyone was in their beds
She dragged her trike upstairs and had a ball
Racing her little bike throughout the halls
She had a zest for living t'was her call
But did her best to conquer all pitfalls
Spending much time inside hospital walls

Hiding her tears she chose instead to please
Excelling in most everything with ease
Water polo for Nora was a breeze
And history, math, and English with some ease
She loved animals everyone agrees
Poppy, Rutgers, and Cricket were her threes

Nora's favorite expression could displease
Never wanting to miss a family soiree
She planned to bake a cake for Granddad's birthday
Seeing St. Peter I think I heard her say

"Oh shit. I was supposed to bring the cake."

CARL BACHELOR

Carl Bachelor was born in Flagler Beach, Florida, and attended school in Jacksonville. He is also a graduate of Antelope Valley College in Lancaster, California. Carl served three years in the U.S. Navy Submarine service, and was employed for forty-five years in aerospace which includes working on the Saturn Apollo Moon Rocket and the Space Shuttle at Kennedy Space Center in Florida. He has been happily married for forty-two years.

Carl's main purpose for writing a story for this anthology is to record the events of the death of his cousin, Gloria Canada, as a tribute to her. It has dwelt in the back of his mind that what he saw years ago may have been about her. He knows that forty-five years is a long time, but he feels it is right to at least raise the question. His thoughts of her have been with him that long, and will remain forever.

TO CANADA FROM US

I was curious and baffled when the Apollo astronauts displayed a banner which read: "TO CANADA FROM US." Commentators and newspaper reporters were also thinking this over because relations with our northern neighbors weren't all that spectacular then.

At that time, I was shuttling back and forth from Florida to California working with Rocketdyne and North American Rockwell on the giant rocket booster. This was about 1969-1970. Like practically everyone else in the United States, I was caught up in the "GO" fever mode of the lunar missions. We had reached our objective to beat the Russians and land on the moon, a milestone that was accomplished in July 1969.

I have been reflecting on these facts some forty-five years and I'm not quite certain about the timing of some events. But while working on the Saturn/Apollo Project, I had the opportunity to be in NASA Headquarters at the Kennedy Space Center, where my cousin Gloria worked as a receptionist.

Gloria was a stunningly beautiful young woman and could have won any beauty pageant if she so chose. I can picture her now, all decked out in her hostess uniform. We talked a little about the old days, and how she could always get a laugh from just about everyone with her pronunciation of the word "yacht." She would say "yatch," like rhymes with "catch." This was symbolic of her and anyone who heard it would remember her.

In December 1970, my stepdad called to give me the bad news that Gloria had been killed in an automobile accident in Satellite Beach. She was only twenty-four years old and left behind her husband and a daughter. I knew her by her maiden name of Gloria Mathis, and had forgotten that she was married and generally known as Gloria Canada.

As Paul Harvey used to say, "And now…the rest of the story." Gloria probably knew familiarly all of the astronauts at one time or another while she worked at NASA Headquarters. I believe that it was a great and final tribute by these heroic Apollo astronauts which would explain the banner they proudly displayed, "TO CANADA FROM US." I have talked to her husband, and he also believes that the banner was in reference to his wife Gloria.

There could be other variations of this story. Maybe the banner meant, "TO CANADA FROM U.S." I am not sure of the periods, and cannot corroborate this because it seems that this part of the video of the moon landing is missing. The closest mission to her death was Apollo 14, January 31, 1971, and two of the three astronauts have now passed away.

My sister lives in Titusville, near the Kennedy Space Center, and reminds me that while it is close to NASA Headquarters, there are many people in the area with the last name Canada. My Mom, Idelle, at the young age of ninety-four is the last of her family and still reminds me to be nice! But I find it hard to let go.

May God bless you cousin. Know that you are not forgotten.

AARON LEWIS

Aaron Lewis grew up in Massachusetts and first attempted writing when he was twelve years old. He returned to his attempts throughout the years with little success. Without realizing what he was doing, he sought numerous careers involved in storytelling. Aaron moved to California and finally, in 2012, he began an earnest attempt at writing a book. He has completed a number of short stories and poems, while still hard at work on that book.

LOST

I am lost.

I have no memory of where I've been and no compass
    to guide me forward.

Have you seen me? Do you know me? Would you
    recognize me as lost?

Frivolity fills my days with no meaning; no purpose. I feel
    blinded by technology.

The universe is at my fingertips, yet all of it is foreign to me.

With no heart, I have no home and so I wander.

I search for an anchor; for something to reel me in.

Who am I? What am I supposed to be doing? Where
    should I be?

Years pass, yet not one second of substance shows itself.

I remain a sojourner ravaged by the emptiness
    that only time reveals.

IN THE BLINK OF A EYE

All she did was blink...really, that's all she did. Now, everything had changed. Her eyes were still hazy since she just woke up. In fact, her head was still on her pillow. Well, it was a moment ago, but now...

Come on, Janie, she thought to herself, *pull your shit together.*

Janie strained to focus her vision, but it all looked like a dream. It had to be a dream. She truly wanted this to be dream, because the reality was extremely disturbing. The longer this persisted, the more uncomfortable she was with her surroundings.

Let's think about this, she examined. *What happened last night?*

She had gone out on a Friday night purely as a dare. Her two co-workers said she would never go since her break up with Seth had only been a week ago, but Janie proved them wrong. Not only did she go, but she had the best time in two years. She had never noticed how much of a downer Seth had been until last night.

Janie had gone to bed somewhere between buzzed and drunk and she was damned sure she was gonna have a crazy hangover in the morning, but didn't imagine that would include visions.

Last night, there had been a fan going, but now it was so hot it felt like a boulder on top of her. The air held an acidic, burning smell and not the usual lavender potpourri. Instead of her apartment's peeling, sailboat wallpaper, Janie's eyes were focused on a wall of layered sand and small rocks. She could hear some commotion going on, but couldn't tell from where.

Janie rolled over in complete disbelief and with an ever-growing desperation for some normalcy. She made it to her back and recognized the blue sky and white clouds (although, they shouldn't be in her bedroom). There was also a black, oily smoke wafting right to left.

Just layin' here is not helping, she said to herself and decided to sit up. Things suddenly got a lot worse.

With the better view of her surroundings, Janie realized she was in a trench. By the looks of it, an Army trench. There were some men dressed in desert camouflage with some sort of weapon by their side. Most sat with their backs up against the trench wall. A few were squatting and one was peering over the top with binoculars to see beyond this microcosm. All of them were wearing helmets which, according to Brian, her enlisted brother, meant some sort of combat was either going on or soon to come.

Taking inventory of the situation was not getting her anywhere. Janie knew what she saw, but had no idea where she was or how she got here.

Maybe I need to talk to someone and find out how I got here...wherever "here" is.

She figured the soldier with the binoculars was either in charge or close by the guy who was. Putting her feet beneath her while maintaining a squat, she began duck walking to her objective.

"Hello!" Janie called out trying to get his attention. He jerked his head to look in her direction and promptly dropped his binoculars. Two soldiers sitting close by grabbed their rifles and quickly directed their working ends at Janie.

"Whoa!" she cried out, placing her hands into a surrender gesture, "I can explain."

The man with the binoculars approached. He had two bars on his lapel which meant he was a captain, and his embroidered name read "Harris."

"Where the hell did *you* come from?" the captain demanded.

Jane thought about that question for a moment and admitted, "That I can't explain. I was hoping you might be able to help."

"What!?" Captain Harris said in utter bewilderment. Janie actually felt a little better now that someone else was sharing this feeling with her.

"Look, all I know is one minute I was lying in my bed. I literally blinked my eyes and I was lying here in this trench."

Captain Harris looked at Janie with a cold stare. She could see he was calculating every word she just said, analyzing it for deception. She knew how it sounded, but it was the truth.

How do you convince someone of the truth when it makes no sense? Her inner voice was offering no help.

"You were lying in bed?" the captain asked to confirm he had heard her correctly.

"That's right," Janie quickly answered.

"Where was that?" he inquired. Captain Harris wanted to get to the bottom of this pronto.

"In my apartment," she offered. Janie wasn't quite sure what the captain was looking for.

Patiently, he added, "And where is your apartment?"

"Oh...Pittsburgh," she explained. Saying "Pittsburgh" and watching the captain's eyes widen, suddenly brought more realism to the situation. She timidly asked, "Where am I now?"

"Afghanistan," Captain Harris offered without breaking his gaze on her.

"How?" Janie uttered. She had a lot of other questions, but her head wouldn't stop spinning long enough for something to come out. The dizziness translated to her body and she wobbled. She toppled forward into the captain's chest.

Captain Harris quickly grabbed her at the shoulders and set her right again. He looked over Janie's shoulder and called out, "Torres, get your ass over here!"

Janie began a fanciful thought about how Torres was her name, too. She stuck with her faraway thought by reminding herself that it wasn't all that odd. After all, Torres is pretty common.

"Torres, what is the problem?" the captain shouted.

"Coming, Sir," was the response heard from behind Janie. She knew that voice and suddenly this bizarre morning was making more sense. Despite the lack of blood pressure in her head, she whipped around to see the familiar face.

"Brian?"

Brian stopped abruptly and cocked his head slightly.

"Janie?" he asked in return, trying to understand. Janie found the confusion was growing every moment. Brian continued his questioning by asking, "How'd you get here?"

"I don't-"

A large explosion came from behind Brian and expanded rapidly. Its force pushed Brian toward Janie and she squeezed her eyes tight merely as a reflex. She anticipated the force to hit her and then,...nothing. In fact, the air was surprisingly still. Then a familiar scent of lavender was detected.

She slowly released the tension in her eyes and as they opened, she was overjoyed by the sight of her bedroom. A reassuring explanation came to her instantly.

"What a crazy friggin' dream!"

She stood in the center of the room and examined everything. It was all there: the old wallpaper, the potpourri pot on her nightstand, even her laptop that she had left open last night after she checked her email. She looked at it again and saw there was a new message.

Dragged her finger lightly across the touchpad, she got to the new message and then clicked on it. It opened and she read:

> Janie,
>
> I'm not sure what the hell is going on, but I need to figure this out. I think you were here, in Afghanistan. In fact, I'd swear you were here. I know that's crazy, but I wasn't the only one who saw you. Two other guys and my captain. Then just after I saw you, there was an explosion from an RPG that hit right where I had been stationed. If you hadn't shown up, I wouldn't be alive to write you now. I was still hit by the explosion, but this body armor we wear protected me enough that I only had the wind knocked out of me. Whatever happened today, I am extremely gratefully. All I know is my baby sister was my guardian angel today. Janie, I don't say this enough...I LOVE YOU!
>
> -Big Bro Bri

Janie read the email again and then once more to be sure. She replayed the last ten minutes in her head. *It had to be real...had to be. But how?* She hadn't noticed, but she had begun to pace, so she walked to her bed to sit down. As she continued, she felt light-headed again. This time, her bed broke her fall. She had a final glimpse of a thought as she lost consciousness.

Where to now?

PUNCTURE

Unsweetened candy makes a heading south
And it tastes so good in parched empty mouth
Tangible red-greens slay imaginings
Directions are soft at the beginnings

The waves of reason crash against the thorn
But the dam is built, reason slashed and torn
So the play begins as the curtain burns
The book wide open as the first page turns

The whitened trees drip upward to the sky
Unnerving drumbeat of your heart asks why
Corners turn away into a smooth sphere
Your shadow shakes hands, shouting "Outta here!"

"Paint my puppies pink!" exclaims the oboe
Skipping green checkers across hot cocoa
All the accusers left their calling card
Their howling has stopped by drowning in lard

Door marked evidence and you perpetrate
Stealing the gold crown from the magistrate
Hearing the laughter encourages it
Listen to the tears causing one more fit

Ground swallows you whole down and down you crawl
Can't ever climb up, but you don't quite fall
Watching the clouds sneeze, the thirteenth hour chime
When will it leave you, a matter of time

The speed quickening and happiness bails
Loose restraint says, "Yes, there's no time for jails"
The cows have come home, the fat lady sings
The end draweth nigh as the sunset stings

The stars in the sky flicker like your thoughts
Your blood still races with each second bought
Faster it all comes, life swirls in your head
Tomorrow, right here, they will find you dead

CARMEN BETANCOURT

Carmen Betancourt is a casting director/producer/talent manager and is on the board of a non-profit organization dedicated to the education and prevention of domestic violence and abuse through film and music. Although fairly new to writing, she has written a short film and a full length film, both of which are in development. She is also currently working on a cookbook that will not only include recipes but also stories of her family. *Food, Family & Fiestas* will be available near the end of 2016.

VACATION THRILLER

The anticipation was killing me. Lying in bed, lights out. I was awake all night, though I tried to sleep. I was tired but the moment my eyes shut, a stream of thoughts ran through my head. Lists, actually. A list of things to do before tomorrow:

–Pay my bills that are due…check.
–Oil change, windshield wipers, air in tires…check, check, check.
–Full tank of gas…check.
–AAA card in my wallet…check.
–Cash (even though I have credit and debit cards)…check.
–Emergency road equipment…check.
–Maps…check.
–Pack medications…check.
–Pack enough clothing for the both of us…check.
–Pack umbrellas, flashlights, matches
    (just in case, of what I don't know)…check, check, check
–All toiletries…check.

Like counting sheep, it finally put me to sleep.
The alarm rang with urgency. My daughter and I sprang to our feet and got started with our morning routine. Usually Amber, an intelligent and funny seven year old, would stay in bed even after she heard the alarm. I would wake her up but she would always say,

78

"Wake me up in fifteen minutes."

Soon she got wise to me and realized that I woke her up earlier to factor in those fifteen minutes. She then added another five to ten minutes to her morning wake up call. Not this day. She was cheerful and wide awake. She was ready for our adventure.

I was a fairly young single mom, twenty-eight years old. I worked hard to support our little family and I needed this time off. Vacation! My only sister, Candy, who is five years my junior, had just bought a new car, so we decided on a road trip. This would be fun.

We filled the trunk with our bags and everything else we thought we might be able to use. We even added things we probably would never use but you never know. In the back seat we had a bag of snacks, a cooler we borrowed, and a bag of things to keep Amber busy on the long drive. She brought her favorite blanket and pillow. We said our good-byes to our parents, but as we were saying good-bye, a bee started buzzing around the passenger side door. It seemed it wanted to join us. We swatted at it and it moved away just long enough for Candy to get in.

We laughed about starting the day with such a close call; a bee sting could have ruined our vacation. We took off. This was the beginning to an exciting adventure. This was the first time we were setting out on our own. We decided to drive up North along the Pacific Coast Highway, stopping wherever we wanted. We were driving from East Los Angeles to San Francisco, then inland to visit my grandmother in Fresno before coming home. We only made hotel reservations in Santa Barbara and in San Francisco, but thought it would be more fun to just stop either when I was tired of driving or when we were someplace so interesting that we wanted to spend more time there. All three of us were excited about our trip.

We were on Interstate 5, transitioned to the 101 and were in Santa Monica; from here we would travel along the Coast. We were all talking, laughing and making plans of places we wanted to see. We planned to stop in Santa Barbara and spend a couple of days there. The plan was to check into the motel, eat breakfast and tour the city. Instead, we stopped near Malibu to have breakfast. It seems that road trips make everyone hungry. After eating a hearty meal, we walked out to the car and were surprised to see that bee still on the antenna. How could that be? My sister was going to swipe it off, but Amber didn't let her.

"Let's see how long it will stay with us," Amber said. We left the bee alone and continued on our way.

We were about a half hour into our drive and Amber was sound asleep in the back seat. My sister was in the same condition in the front seat. I kept trying to wake them up.

"Hey, wake up. You're missing the scenery," I said. I just heard a lot of grumbling from the front and back seats. They finally woke up when I turned the motor off. I was parked in the parking lot of the motel where we would stay.

Candy opened her eyes, looked around and said, "We're here already? That was quick."

We checked into the motel; nothing special but it was clean and in a good area. Amber didn't care where we were as long as it had a swimming pool.

We unpacked what we needed, freshened up and went walking around the city, drove to the beach and checked out the shops. We went back to the motel, took a little rest and changed for dinner. The restaurant was upscale with delicious food. Amber was impressed and I don't think the restaurant served too many seven year olds. She was very well behaved and used her best manners. We did a little more walking and returned to the motel. It was time for bed.

The next day we woke up, re-packed the car and were off. Snacks were opened. The weather was great. We drove up the coast, passing San Luis Obispo and Morro Bay. The ocean was blue and forceful as it crashed against the rocks, spraying white droplets into the air. It was a beautiful sight, although I was the only one that saw it. My two companions were fast asleep.

I stopped the car at San Simeon. One of the things that we wanted to do was see Hearst Castle. The sign said "Closed for repairs." Just my luck. We drove a little further north, having lunch at a cute little restaurant with a terrific ocean view. We drove on after lunch. They were asleep again and I was alone.

Since they were asleep, I made the decision to drive as much as I could. It was late afternoon and soon the sun would set. It was pretty quiet, no traffic to speak of. The ocean on one side and the mountains on the other. What more could one ask for, besides companions that were awake to share it with. I reflected on the fact that we were two young women with a child, driving alone in an unpopulated area that seemed to go on forever.

What if something happened? What if we got a flat tire or something? There were no phones. I just wanted out of the area. I was scaring myself. I've always had a vivid imagination. There was nowhere to stop, but did I really want to? Not really. I was tired and anxious but tried to stay calm. After all, I was in charge; I was responsible for the safety of the two sleepy heads that had no idea I was afraid. I had to keep a level head. When would I get to the next town?

It was evening when we arrived in Carmel. Yes, I was relieved. I woke the sleeping beauties, but naturally, I didn't tell them what was going through my head on the drive. I didn't want them to worry or worse yet, start thinking the way I was thinking. This was to be a fun adventure.

We walked through the little town of quaint shops, and interesting restaurants. We wanted to stay in the area to take advantage of all Carmel had to offer. I looked for a motel in the area but only came across expensive hotels. I didn't want to spend too much; we still had more travel days to go. I figured if I drove a little further from town, there should be less expensive places to sleep. It was night when we continued on our way towards Monterrey Bay. There was a large building lit up with twinkle lights so we headed that way. We stopped to see what it was. I was hoping for a restaurant and maybe a motel close by. It was actually a merry-go-round. Amber was thrilled. She rode a horse that went up and down. We bought candy and souvenirs. It was getting late now and we needed two things; dinner and a place to sleep. We found a place for a seafood dinner on the pier. After dinner we walked a little, but I was tired and worried about finding a place to stay. I asked around and was told that just outside of Monterrey we should be able to find something, perhaps in Pacific Grove.

I was exhausted. The first place we stopped had no vacancies. The road was extremely dark and quiet, but I could see lights ahead. As we got closer, we could see little cabins and a sign that said "Vacancy." This is where we would stay. I turned into the narrow driveway and parked in front of the office. A hefty woman in her late fifties came to the desk. She wore jeans and a work shirt, hair pulled back, no make-up. She looked like she had put in a hard day's work, possibly for many years. She was friendly, welcomed us and said that she only had the large cabin in the back available.

It cost more than I wanted to spend. When she saw my daughter and how tired we were, she offered it at a lesser price.

I paid her, took the key and thanked her. She gave us directions on how to get back there. Once we passed the office, the area was much larger than it seemed. However, it was so dark it was hard to see much. We parked the car in the designated location next to the cabin. We grabbed our bags, opened the door and trudged right through.

It was rustic but very clean. The living room area was a good size with a large fireplace, and was open to a dining area and the kitchen. The kitchen was stocked with appliances, including a coffeemaker. Down the hall were four doors. One was to the bedroom with two full size beds; across the hall was a bathroom with a shower and bathtub. One of the other doors on the same side of the hallway was a large closet, and the last door against the wall at the end of the hallway was…locked. Why was it locked? Maybe it was for storage.

I was too tired to think about it. We put our bags in the room. Candy and I went back to the car to get the cooler my dad lent us. We wanted the drinks that were in it…water, cokes and juice. We took that into the kitchen. We all changed into our pajamas. Even though it was late and we were tired, we got our drinks and sat in the living room for a bit. We finally went to bed, but it was too quiet, we are after all, city girls. I turned the radio on, turned the volume to low. Amber fell asleep (she was an expert at it), and Candy and I talked for a little while.

I drifted off to a good night's rest. Suddenly, I woke up to a strange noise, it sounded like it was coming from the living room. I tried to summon the courage to go see what it was, but every horror movie I had ever seen came to mind. "Don't go out there alone." I didn't want to scare anyone, so I got out of bed. My sister must have heard me, and then she also heard the strange noise. We went into the living room. The noise was coming from the kitchen. It sounded like scraping and squeaking and someone walking like they were trying to be quiet. My sister was scared and so was I.

I just kept thinking it was up to me to keep us safe. The noise persisted and I wasn't sure what to do. I am not going outside, people get killed that way. I'll call the desk. I knew the woman would probably be upset but I didn't know what else to do. It was probably nothing so I didn't want to call the police.

"What's the name of this place?" I asked Candy.

"I don't know," she answered. "You checked in."

I was so tired and happy to have found someplace to sleep that I hadn't really paid attention. The key should have the name of the place; got the key...no name. The receipt was in my purse, still no name. The noise was getting louder or maybe that was just in my head. I must be starring in a horror film.

Candy checked on Amber; she was still asleep. When Candy came back into the living area, (I hoped that wouldn't become ironic), she was holding a Swiss Army knife. I had no idea where she got it from but I was glad she had it. She found me looking through the yellow pages. I knew the street we were on so I thought to look through the section on Motels-Cabins, all the while there could be a murderer just feet away. Somehow I found the number and called. One ring, two rings, three rings and finally someone answered. I hurriedly explained what was happening; I'm sure I sounded panicked. I could hear her smile over the phone. She sounded eerily friendly and calm.

"Don't worry dear, that's just a raccoon at the sliding glass door. That pesky raccoon comes everyday looking for food. The people that stayed there previously fed him, even though I told them not to. The cabin you're in butts up against the forest. You never know what kind of creatures will come out of the forest."

I felt relieved, foolish but somehow still a little frightened. We went back to our beds and tried to get some well-deserved rest.

I was drifting off when I heard voices. The noise from the kitchen was louder but now I heard muffled voices. Where were they coming from? I could hear the voices in the hallway, a little louder but still indistinguishable. I grabbed my sister's knife from the night stand, pulling the blade out. I thought it would protect us from the intruders but it was short and very dull, the equivalent to a butter knife. The voices had an eerie and haunting quality. My imagination was in overdrive. I couldn't breathe. Was this place haunted?

I said a silent prayer but before I could finish, my sister sat straight up in bed and stared at me with fright on her face. We looked at each other, not knowing what to do. The voices were low: one male, the other female. They seemed to be arguing. What do we do? There was a muffled crash, then silence. Heavy breathing, was it them, was it Candy or me? I knew from past experience, I believed in ghosts. Whether this was real or not, I knew we had to leave now.

We quickly dressed and threw everything into our bags. Only a couple of hours before sunrise, but we were not waiting. I woke Amber up and told her we had to leave. She couldn't understand why and I was not going to tell her. Still in her pajamas, she got into the car. We threw the bags into the trunk and were about to leave when Candy remembered our dad's cooler. I knew he would be upset if we left it. He would not believe the ghost story. So with the motor running, I ran back inside. While I was in there I heard a scream. I ran out dragging the cooler, shoved it in the back seat and drove off. My heart was pounding; Candy was white as a ghost, but Amber was asleep once again.

We did continue our trip and thankfully the rest of the vacation was not as exciting. It was fun and relaxing. By the way, the bee stayed on the antenna the whole week and did not fall off until we were at home and parked in the drive way.

I told this story to my friend that lives in Carmel and knew of the cabins in Pacific Grove. When I went to visit many years later, we took a ride over there. We drove to the back to see the cabin where it all took place. I walked around the cabin in the light of day and realized that the door that had been locked at the end of the hallway was to an adjoining room at the end of the cabin.

ADRIANA ALEXANDER

Adriana Alexander grew up in Buffalo, New York, and she is the talented daughter of AVWA member, Patricia Alexander. She began writing poems and songs when she was five years old. Her love of writing, singing, and acting inspired her to study English literature, creative writing, and theater at State University of New York at Buffalo. After college she moved to Southern California to pursue a career in the entertainment world. Adriana belongs to the Screen Actors Guild and has performed on television and in numerous films. She enjoys singing her original songs and has performed with her band in Los Angeles, New York City, and Las Vegas.

Adriana is also a naturopathic doctor and has recently completed her PhD in Natural Health Sciences. She writes a daily health blog and is currently writing a book about anti-aging, as well as another which is a collection of her poems.

TELEVISION

Hypnotic vision

Electric incision

Mental division

You no longer envision

We make your decision

We are Television

85

THE LIVING DEAD

The living are the dead

That eat what they are fed.

Swallow the spoon of sorrow

Sugar-coated to taste so sweet.

Then pop a pill to numb and march

To that constipated horror beat.

Eat up the bowl of GMO lies.

You can't see the mirrored eyes

Floating in the drowning milk,

Watching you as you chew.

Fish genetics in your berries,

Without a label you have no clue.

Mother Nature has been raped

Disfiguring genetics taking shape. . .

Everyone keeps dancing to the Zombie song,

Munching on poison as they sing-a-long.

BEHOLDER OF MAGIC

The top of the Eucalyptus giants sway
They bend in the twilight breeze.
So faintly the wind ignites fingerlike leaves,
Awakening their perfume and majestic dance
An ancient tribal tree dance.
The Dance of the Calling.

A waltzing séance ensues to the tranquil rhythm of the crickets,
As the dancing giants summon their King,
Spirits rise as he glides into his throne.
He swoops down on silent wing with ghostly grace.
The Beholder of Magic, The Great Horned Owl
Ruler of the High Forest

He calls out into the gloaming, into the perfect calm.
Hooting his mantra to the forest creatures,
An eerie narcotic call echoes through the trees
Hypnotically soothing them into an unsuspecting slumber.
His spell is cast....his round eyes glow like rolling crystal balls
reflecting the fading light.

His Majesty fluffs his feathers and pointed tufts upon his head.
He readies himself for his second serenade.
Again he sings,
"Hoot, hoot, hoot, hoooo...hoooo...hoooot..."
He looks directly down at me awaiting my response.
Our eyes meet and I feel a soul connection with this wildling.

I take a deep breath and perform my best great horned owl call.
I stand still, patiently waiting, wondering what he must think of
This very large featherless, flightless Owl-like being below him.
The seconds click caterpillar-slow, inching alongside my anticipation.
His silence breaks as he copies my Owl call!
I am elated as I prepare to respond.

The Great Horned Owl and I enjoy our hoot hooting
Communication for twenty minutes.
I feel honored and blessed to be accepted into
the magical fold of the Forest King.

MONTENEGRO

The blue black mountains of Montenegro touch the sky. The green growth of Spring veins through the majestic rock pulsing with new life, painting a labyrinth winding upwards.

While herding his goats and sheep, the boy searches the sky hoping to find his eagle. He misses him dearly after the long harsh winter. He walks along the white limestone bed of the Piva River as it snakes through ravines. The boy stops so he and his animals can drink from the pure turquoise water.

As he leads his herd through high canyon passes, he hollers out, "Drago!" His hope filled voice echoes for miles through the natural amphitheater of Mount Durmitor. He waits then calls out again, "Drago! Drago!" He is determined to find his eagle.

Finally his calls are answered! He sees his eagle soaring overhead! The thick wool coat his mother knitted him is perfect for this occasion. He stretches his arm out and hardens his muscles like a tree branch as he calls again, "Drago!"

Drago circles overhead then swoops yellow talons down and lands on the boy's arm with perfect grace. The boy is overjoyed to see his best friend again. He gently strokes Drago's beautiful brown feathered body and feeds him a lizard that he caught for this special occasion. The boy talks to his eagle with great affection.

The boy first discovered Drago two summers ago when the eagle was very young. Drago had been caught in a rain storm and the boy found him in the valley with a wounded wing. The boy brought the eagle home and with great care and instruction from his mother, nursed Drago back to his magnificence. The eagle never forgot.

While nursing Drago, the boy remembered how he himself had been injured and left for dead a few years before. During the war, his mother was protecting and caring for American soldiers that had crashed their plane and landed within trees in Montenegro. The soldiers lived with the boy's family within the caves of Durmitor to hide from the Nazis. The boy's mother asked him to fetch water from the river. He and his cousin snuck down to the water's edge to fill their buckets. The boy heard two loud shots.

A Nazi shot him in the lower leg and his cousin was shot in the chest and died on top of him. The boy blacked out. When he awoke, he was in his mother's arms back in the cave.

Luckily the bullet passed through his leg, and his mother dressed the wound and treated him with healing herbs from the mountains. The boy recovered completely and was able to run again. He thanked God and was grateful for his recovery.

When the boy found the young wounded eagle, he wanted to give Drago the second chance at life he himself had been granted. He gave Drago unwavering love and care so he too could fly again.

COYOTE PACK

A wild bark breaks into a cackling howl in the canyon below

The coyotes have awakened from their den

Crunching leaves and breaking twigs as they come closer

Hungry blue flame eyes appear on the trail

Catching the light in my hand

Glowing orbs swirling

Watching me from afar

First two, then four, six, then eight

Iridescent circles dancing....

Camouflage beige and brown fur bodies

Huddled up against wild oak and forest green

Drenched in cerulean twilight

Fear strikes me but I am brave and stay on my path

The hunters are waiting for me to pass

To resume their search for rabbit and deer

INTERTWINED

Exploration of aura
Senses stimulate
They pulse to the chemical interaction
Of you and I.
Energy fields mesh
As threads are intertwined like
Fishnet on the gartered legs
Taunt with anticipation of releasing disrobe.
And disrobe we do
With all clothes remaining
Shedding the defenses
The stonewall of the soul.

Let down the veil
Reveal a layer of truth.

ANGEL: A SONG FOR FRANCO

You're Hot because you are
My Angel of Fire
I see the Flame is in your eyes
Oh - you are burning a
Path to my door
Never knew Love like this before

You are my Heaven
My Angel of Fire
I see the Sun behind your eyes
Oh- I hear you melting through
My lock and chain
Now you hold the key to my door

WILMA WEBSTER

Wilma Webster graduated from UCLA and then moved to Mexico with her husband. She stayed in Mexico for fifteen years where she studied Medicine while raising her family. Wilma was an emergency physician for sixteen years. She joined the U.S. Army reserves and served her country in Saudi Arabia during Desert Storm. She then switched to the U.S. Air Force, serving in Japan, England, Panama, South Korea, and finally Nebraska. Wilma returned to school and earned a Masters in HR and Psychology.

During her service and careers, Wilma discovered a talent for writing. She edited the *Columbia County Medical Society Medical Bulletin* from 1989-1992. In Panama, she wrote medical articles for the AFB newspaper, and compiled a booklet, *Wellness Wisdom*, which was distributed to base personnel. From 2008 to 2011 she was the editor of *Chai Desert News*, a monthly newsletter.

Wilma is currently raising a grandchild and working on her memoirs. She loves getting help from the Antelope Valley Writers Association.

THE LAMPOON

It was the end of our Internal Medicine residency. After three years of hard work and many hours of study, being 'on call' every third night, studying *ad infinitum* every possible alteration of an EKG tracing, and refining the insertion of subclavian catheters and pacemakers, there was finally ample reason to celebrate.

As per hospital tradition, our merrymaking would take the form of a "Lampoon," an occasion for graduating resident physicians to publicly poke fun at their teachers, the slave masters of the previous three years. It was a good release of tension when most needed, a respite along the path of our difficult journey. The audience knew what to expect, and they had been provided with noisemakers to assist in the gaiety.

No sooner had the emcee welcomed the attendees, when I quickly and surreptitiously stuffed a pillow inside my dress. Looking very pregnant, I called out to the master of ceremonies, demanding to speak to one of the attending physicians by name, and accusing him of being the father of my unborn child. It took intense self-control to keep a straight face, but when I had finished speaking the audience was in stitches!

We sang well-known songs with new lyrics, putting a teacher's name in place of "Old Man River," for example. We performed a skit where we did CPR to the theme music of *The Lone Ranger*. I played the part of a patient wearing a sexy negligee, poised to jerk my body upwards as soon as my 'doctors' pretended to shock my heart into a normal rhythm. And when women came up to the podium to perform, whoever was in charge of the spotlight would focus it on the most interesting parts of their anatomy, causing additional laughter.

Understand that the seriousness of our jobs and the huge amount of stress involved fully justified to us this one night of frivolity. We sang songs about our teachers, the work, and even about the diseases we studied, diagnosed, and treated.

One of the conditions, idiopathic hypertrophic sub-aortic stenosis (IHSS), is a cause of sudden cardiac death at all ages, particularly among young athletes, who are frequently screened for the disease. The name is a real mouthful and particularly hard to memorize, so we'd been taught a song as a good mnemonic device, and we included it in the Lampoon, sung to the tune of the *Mary Poppins* song, "Supercalifragilisticexpialidocious":

> Idiopathic hypertrophic sub-aortic stenosis
> Propranolol and surgery after diagnosis,
> But even with the best of care, there's still a poor prognosis.
> Idiopathic hypertrophic sub-aortic stenosis.

After my residency, I did not continue with Internal Medicine because I found it somewhat boring, but I went on to work as an emergency physician, first in New York, and then Pennsylvania. Medicine was a serious proposition, and I soon forgot the glee of the Lampoon.

But years later, now retired in a suburb of Los Angeles, I was sitting comfortably at a Starbucks table when I overheard a conversation from an adjacent table that suddenly brought back the Lampoon days.

A young man was telling his companion how he'd wanted all his life to be a professional baseball player, and now that it was within his reach, he'd been rejected because of some weird diagnosis: idiopathic hypertrophic sub-aortic stenosis. He had no idea what it was and why it could have derailed his plans so badly.

"Pardon me for interrupting," I said, "but I heard you mention idiopathic hypertrophic sub-aortic stenosis, or IHSS, which I've studied in the past. You're lucky they caught it because it can make you very, very sick. When I was a medical resident, we even learned a song about it to help us study the condition. If you want, I'll bring you more information and I'll even copy the song for you."

He was interested, so that night I searched for the VHS tape of the Lampoon and taped the song for him. In so doing I actually listened to it, and my heart sank when I realized how callous it was to sing so gaily about such a deadly illness. I also went online and visited the Mayo Clinic site and copied their pamphlet for patients with the disease. I met him the next day and gave all the information to him, apologizing for my insensitivity and wishing him the best with a very difficult diagnosis.

Addendum:

On the Mayo Clinic site about hypertrophic cardiomyopathy, a broad category of cardiac muscle enlargement that includes IHSS and others, it says: "Hypertrophic cardiomyopathy [HCM], while usually not fatal in most people, is the most common cause of heart-related sudden death in people under 30. It's the most common cause of sudden death in athletes. HCM often goes undetected." *

* http://www.mayoclinic.org/sudden-death/art-20047571.

JOY OF BAND-AIDS

It was another chance to show I could raise children well, because my own had not turned out as perfectly as I had planned. At my request, little Steven stayed with me from Monday through Friday, and weekends he would spend with his mom. Steven is my grandchild, the child of my youngest son.

I put Steven in a nursery school where they began teaching him the ABC's. Supplementing that with a daily class at home, I had him reading on his own by age five, and doing rudimentary algebra (like x plus x equals 2x). He got a weekly allowance of $15 for doing his daily lessons, and always saved up his earnings.

Having gotten a Master's Degree in psychology a few years beforehand, I knew all about the new parenting techniques. Teaching children to respect others by showing *them* respect really made a difference, as did other techniques such as having family meetings for all to negotiate and sign contracts for house rules.

I was very pleased at how little Steven was turning out, but sometimes we had minor problems, like when he hurt himself and started 'the Band-Aid era.' The first small bandage elicited a lot of attention from adults, who huddled around to say, "Ooh, you have a boo-boo! How did that happen?"

All kids love attention, and soon little Steven was requesting a Band-Aid for every small bump and bruise. When visitors came and saw him covered in bandages they would ask, genuinely alarmed, "What happened to him?"

What could I answer? After quite a bit of thought and discussion, I decided on the correct answer: "It's a fashion statement!" That made things clear, but soon thereafter I found it necessary to issue an edict to Steven: "There must be at least a drop of blood to get a Band-Aid."

Things seemed to work better after that, and life settled back to normal. Days were getting cooler with Chanukah coming around the corner. What could I get for my precocious 5 ½ year old? Thinking of what I would have wanted at his age, I bought two different science kits: one for growing crystals, and another to help budding amateur botanists examine plants. Then, for a more toy-like gift, and following the modern parenting pattern, I thought it would be best to ask *him* what he most wanted for the holiday.

The answer came much faster than I had expected, obviously something he had in his mind for quite a while. "What I want most for Chanukah? That's easy . . . BAND-AIDS!"

I should have known better, but somehow his answer was a total surprise. I felt as if I was tricking him; it was my denial of Band-Aids, after all, that led to his desire. I had been expecting him to give the name of an action toy, or other expensive plaything, but of all things, not Band-Aids!

I got to work on it immediately and bought Band-Aids with every cartoon character or super-hero I could find: Scooby-Doo, Sponge Bob, Superman, Batman, and others, lots of them. When he opened the presents the science kits got very little reaction. To this day, I'm not sure if he even opened the boxes. He was overjoyed, however, with the packages of Band-Aids; it was *just* what he wanted!

Epilogue:

I felt so guilty for getting off easily that holiday season, that ever since, Steven has had all the Band-Aids he wants. His interest has indeed waned, but to this day, all he needs to do is open up the Band-Aid drawer.

POOR JOHNNY

I was the big older sister bully,
My little brother was always blamed fully,
The cake in the fridge had layers numbering three,
The middle one, we suddenly couldn't see.
Who could have done this terrible misdeed?
To find out who, just follow my lead.

Johnny is to blame for everything all the time,
Mother come and spank him for his crime.
Who, with a straw, sucked the pudding down an inch?
The answer to that is really quite a cinch.
I'm getting fatter, but Johnny's guilty again,
Give him another spanking for this sin.

My brother was outwitted every time,
We smarter ones don't pay for any crime,
But my ball and chain are extra pounds tonight,
The price I pay for not treating Johnny right.

A darling child, who hadn't yet learned to read,
Johnny one day had a sudden surge of greed,
He stole from Grandpa, yet he paid a horrible price,
You know next time he'll think about it twice.
In Grandpa's desk there was tasty chewing gum,
Johnny took it and tried to keep his deed mum,
Impossible, because he chewed several packs,
Not Wrigley's or Bazooka, Gramp's favorite: Ex-Lax!

THE BOXING SMOKER

Stationed at Howard AFB, Panama, we were setting up a hospital to take over the work of the large Gorgas Hospital which was being closed down. At the end of the year, the canal would be left in Panama's control and all support from the U.S. would be taken over by the Panamanians.

I worked in the Emergency Department, evaluating and treating patients with multiple complaints and ruling out more serious problems which might have to be transported away. This was done in 12-hour shifts more or less every three days, alternating with the other emergency physicians.

Against the backdrop of all that serious hard work, word came out that the Department of Morale and Recreation was sponsoring a 'Boxing Smoker' and needed a physician volunteer for the event. The term 'smoker' is a technical term for the type of boxing match it was, one less formal than professional or amateur matches. It sounded fun and interesting, so I raised my hand, not fully aware of what my responsibilities would entail. I assumed what I would have to do most was to stand by and check out injuries sustained during the match, and evaluate and treat them as needed.

It wasn't long before I learned that I would first have to do the many physical exams on the potential boxers to see if they qualified. Easy enough. I'd done lots of physical exams before, but what I learned next really surprised me.

It seems that to follow the rules of the Amateur Boxing Association, I had to make sure the boxers had two of those things men have two of down below. It wasn't beyond my scope of training; I'd handled an STD clinic before and checked many men for venereal disease, but checking testicles on young boxers was what I had least expected the day I volunteered for that job.

I wasn't the only surprised person. When the boxers came for their exams they, too, were surprised, even fearful, when they saw a female physician! The white coat, stethoscope, and professional demeanor helped allay their fears, but not completely.

All of the young men, while nervous at first, checked out all right, although one had a penile piercing that I had to consult another physician about. We asked him to remove the jewelry during the actual boxing for fear that it could lead to an injury.

By the time the boxing match began, ninety percent of my work was already done. The match went smoothly except for a few minor injuries, and the Boxing Smoker was deemed a success.

Months later, with the boxing match forgotten, the rock group Ten Thousand Maniacs came to play at our base. There I was enjoying the music and dancing disco-style by myself with no care in the world in the midst of the crowd, when several men suddenly pointed at me and yelled, "She touched us, she touched us!"

"No, I didn't," I was quick to yell back.

"Yes, you did," they insisted.

I had been dancing pretty wildly at the crowded concert, but I didn't think I'd touched anyone else. After quite a few awkward moments, it became apparent they had been my boxer patients and in fact, I had touched them. In the end, I had to confess, but then what else was there to do but settle down and continue enjoying the music.

STEVE ORDWAY

Steve Ordway's honorable career as a fireman with the Los Angeles City Fire Department spanned twenty-five years, twelve of which were spent as a paramedic on an ambulance. He had the distinction of being one of the first paramedic firefighters with the L.A. City Fire Department due to a shortage of civilian paramedics, and he was detailed to work on a rescue ambulance for most of his assigned shifts.

Steve's many experiences responding to emergency calls in South Central Los Angeles and Hollywood have provided material for hundreds of tales, some hilarious, some touching, and some on the grisly side (so readers consider yourself forewarned). Steve's wife encouraged him to write about these incidents, which he is compiling into a book on the day-to-day life of a Los Angeles fireman.

AUTO VS. POLE

There it was. A brand new, bright red Corvette with three occupants - wrapped around a power pole. It was the worst thing I had ever encountered in three years on the job. I had been to fires and traffic accidents, and I felt like a veteran fireman when we got the call.

It was an early summer evening when we were dispatched to the traffic accident in the west San Fernando Valley. It soon would be dark as we rolled up the avenue. There were no homes on this wide isolated street, though an exclusive housing tract paralleled it. The nearest houses were 100 yards away, but a crowd had gathered, drawn by what must have been a loud crash. It had been a hot weekend day, and the onlookers had the appearance of having had their barbecues disrupted by the accident - men holding beer cans, women with children, and all were clad in shorts, sandals, or poolside attire.

The three male passengers were crowded into the vehicle's only seat. Two lads in their late teens were on the outside, one hanging out the partially opened passenger door, with an adult astride the console in the middle. As I brought a loaded one-inch protection line up to the event there was a gasoline spill.

I had to push my way through the crowd. The captain ordered them to stand back, and they complied, except for a father holding his young son who implored our skipper, "Can we come closer? My son's never seen a dead body?" His request was denied.

A distraught man who identified himself as a physician informed us that the driver, his nephew, was dead, as was his brother, the man in the middle. The boy on the passenger side, his son, was still alive.

Rescue Ambulance 100 arrived on scene and tried to extricate the son, but that was the side that had hit the pole, pinning his legs. Both of his femurs were obviously broken and bent at a grotesque angle. I stood guard with the hose line as the rest of the crew and rescue ambulance personnel extricated the patient. One of the firemen pushed on the middle man's shoulder, causing the body to rock forward, and as his face dangled down his chest, the top of his skull dropped into his lap. An obviously intoxicated observer who was clutching a half quart beer can, then approached the driver's side, leaned over to peer into the man's open skull, and exclaimed, "My God!" Then he staggered off into the crowd. I probably should have yelled at him, but I was too shocked to move or utter a sound.

About this time two women arrived. One was the wife of the man in the center, and she was also the mother of the teenager in the driver's seat - the two men who were deceased. The other woman was the mother of the boy being extricated; she was the doctor's wife. I have got to hand it to that doctor. He had it together enough to restrain the hysterical ladies before they got close enough to witness the carnage. Before the rescue ambulance left, the engineer grabbed a pillow case and pulled it over the shoulders of the deceased adult in the middle. He said he had to do it as the sight was making him sick. I was so thankful that he did.

It was getting dark, but the crowd remained after the rescue transported the boy. The tow truck was now on scene and provided additional entertainment for the onlookers as it unwrapped the Corvette from the pole so the remaining two bodies could be removed.

I was rendered numb when we learned that the Corvette was a college graduation gift from the doctor to his son. The son had let his teenage cousin have the wheel, and they went for a joy ride. The boy's uncle rode in the middle to keep an eye on the lads. The son, the only one alive at the scene, expired at the hospital.

PRECIOUS

We had just put a clean sheet on our gurney after having delivered a traffic accident patient to the E.R. We were rolling it down the hallway toward the exit doors of the hospital. Entering were two police officers escorting two bedraggled looking individuals.

The pants on the disheveled men were tattered. Their legs and sneakers exhibited dried blood. As we passed them we observed their hands were cuffed behind their backs. Shredded would be the best word to describe the condition of their hands and shirt sleeves.

"What it is, bro?" I inquired, using the street jargon of the men in blue.

One of the officers stopped to relate this story as his partner conducted the prisoners onward for medical treatment.

"We happened upon this car which fit the description of one involved in a burglary. We ran the plate and, sure enough, it came back stolen. We hit the reds and, after a short pursuit, they pulled over, blocking an alley, and then they booked on down there on foot.

We gave chase being forced to leave our black and white on the street. We saw them enter through a gate into a backyard. Then we heard a door slam as they entered a garage that faced the alley.

We're a K-9 unit. See this garage door opener device on my belt? It controls the rear window on our squad car. I simply pressed the button, releasing Precious, our hundred pound bundle of kick-ass. We leashed Precious and stood outside the back door of the garage.

My partner yelled out, 'Come out or we'll send the dog in.'

Silence.

'We have a police dog. Come on out or we'll send her in.'

Still nothing.

My partner kicked the door in, and I released our Precious weapon. There was growling and snarling, accompanied by shouts and screams as Precious counseled the miscreants on their evil deeds. Soon the two men tumbled out in a submissive posture and we called off the dog."

"Sounds like Precious has earned a dog biscuit," I said.

"Oh, she's had her treat; she's the best partner we could ever have. And Precious really enjoys her work," he replied.

We passed the squad car on the way to our ambulance. There was a lot of tail wagging going on inside.

101

CHINGASO

It was a warm summer afternoon when we were dispatched to an assault at an upscale Mexican restaurant located on Ventura Boulevard amid the exclusive shopping section of the San Fernando Valley. We wended our way through the huge crowded parking lot with only our flashing lights, having cut off the siren before entering from a side street.

A commotion was in progress at the entrance to the restaurant. When we were about fifty yards away a young man in his twenties turned, spotted our ambulance, and immediately fell to the ground.

Once on scene, we went first to check his status. He presented the fluttering eyelid syndrome of someone faking unconsciousness. When Vinny, my partner, inquired what the emergency was, the prone individual, I'll call him Jeremy, bounded to his feet and irately began castigating the management and employees of the establishment.

While Vinny was subject to this torrent of indignation, a police car pulled up and an officer then became the target of Jeremy's remonstrations, rescuing my partner from further abuse.

The story related by the manager to the second officer and myself was less self serving than what I heard from the outraged patron. It seems that when Jeremy arrived for dinner with his wife, young son and daughter, he appeared in a foul mood and his first order was a pitcher of margaritas. The alcohol failed to lighten his mood. In fact, he became rude to the waiter, obnoxious to the busboy, and loud and disruptive to the restaurant patrons. His poor wife seemed thoroughly cowed by his conduct. His children sat silently with big eyes watching the fearful action.

The busboy, who the manager said had come in looking for work and had been hired that very day, took exception to the insulting behavior. There hadn't been time to get his name or information as yet, claimed the manager.

"*Bastante,*" the busboy exclaimed as he delivered a *chingaso* to Jeremy's mouth *con mucho gusto*. Jeremy went down on the carpet and rolled around briefly. As the busboy strolled away he muttered "*pendejo!*" There was a brief round of approval from the patrons which did nothing to improve Jeremy's mood.

"My kids saw that. He punched me and got away with it," railed the aggrieved party. "It wasn't a fair fight. They won't see that I'm a real man."

Procuring the loud mouth's drivers license, one of the officers consulted the computer in the police car, then asked Jeremy to step away from the group. Still indignant, he refused to stop berating everyone in sight.

"I'm thinking of how that low life busboy sucker-punching me will affect my children," he raged.

"Then turn around with your hands behind your back. You have warrants," said the officer. "You're going to jail."

As we cleared the scene we saw the kids having to watch their dad get handcuffed and led to the squad car.

FRANCES SERESERES

Frances "Fran" Sereseres was born in Los Angeles. She relocated to the high desert of Lancaster, California, where she and her husband were successful business owners for close to thirty-five years. Fran also worked in the entertainment industry, having appeared in several movies.

Ten years ago, Fran fell and crushed her back and, as a result, now uses a motorized wheelchair. However, this setback has not prevented her from becoming a speaker for those who cannot or will not speak for themselves. She advocates for the seniors and homeless in Lancaster, speaking regularly at city and county meetings on their behalf. For her advocacy, she has received a Certificate of Recognition from the Lancaster City Council and Mayor's Office.

Fran has decided to write her memoirs for her three daughters, four grandchildren, and one soon to arrive great-grandchild.

LITTLE BIRD

It was a nice balmy evening and my husband, our daughter, Melissa, and I went to Sylmar Shopping Center to get ice cream. As we walked, passing the different stores, we were not in any hurry. We walked by the pet shop and decided to go in and look at the puppies, fish, and other animals.

At the rear of the store was a big room which was transformed into an aviary. As we walked into this room we noticed the walls were lined with bird cages with a variety of species. There were parakeets, canaries, love birds, and these birds were all so cute. In the corner was a big cage. As we walked closer we heard a very loud squawk. And as we neared, the squawks got louder and louder. There in the corner of the cage was a Red-lored Amazon Parrot. The owner of the shop said to us that the parrot liked our daughter because his eyes got larger and turned a bright orange color. As my daughter got closer he started to walk around the cage and flutter his feathers.

The sales girl told us that the parrot was from the Los Angeles Zoo. His owner was the curator of the aviary and told her that the parrot was a male. The reason she mentioned this was that they have to be surgically examined to determine their gender. This type of parrot is native to tropical regions of the Americas from Eastern Mexico to south of Ecuador. The plumage is primarily green with red forehead and yellow cheeks.

So after getting all the information and statistics on the bird, we left. We weren't there to get a bird anyway.

We went home, but the conversation continued about the parrot. Melissa was saying how much she liked it and how fun it would be to train him to talk and sit on our shoulders. The conversation came up many times for a couple of days.

My husband and I decided to buy the bird for Melissa since her birthday was coming, but with the understanding that she would be totally responsible for it. We went back to the pet store and the parrot was still available. We bought him at a cost of $380.00. We forgot that we needed a cage and that was another $80.00. Thank goodness it included a branch for a perch as everything was extra. We also needed bird food, a bird water container, and bowls which were another $25.00 plus tax. The ending cost was over $500.00.

We were told that parrots cannot be near drafts or exposed to a lot of sun. They need partial sun. This created another problem. Anyway, we were home now with all the bird's paraphernalia. The first thing was to name him, and Melissa liked Little Bird because of Big Bird from Sesame Street.

Next question was where to put him. Well, we finally decided that the dining area window was a good place. It had limited sunshine and no draft, plus we could enjoy watching him there.

We left him alone for a few days to let Little Bird get acclimated to his surroundings. We then tried to train him by getting him on our shoulders. Well, he went on my daughter's shoulder, but with reservations. He slowly went up my husband's arm and mine.

After days passed, he was still in the training process and we decided to let him perch outside the cage during the day, which he liked. He would walk down the sides of the cage and then back up to the top and would look out the window.

One day, my daughter and I were in the bathroom with the door closed and I was washing her hair. Well, she and I began to play around showing our karate skills whooping and hollering. Melissa was taking classes and was a green belt at the time. Anyway, as we opened the bathroom door, who do you think was right outside the door waiting for us? Well, it was Little Bird. He came after me with a vengeance to bite me. He thought I was hurting Melissa and was going to defend her. Little Bird actually chased me down the hall, until my husband was able to get him with a towel.

Since then, I've been on his blacklist. In my observation of him I noticed that when the TV was on with children on the screen, he would go to the TV, look up, and his eyes would get big and orange. That meant that he enjoyed hearing them.

One day there was a program on in which a child was crying. You should have seen how Little Bird reacted to this. He walked back and forth on the floor and squawked and murmured. He tried to get on the table next to the TV to help the crying child but he couldn't because the table was a plexiglass cube. He couldn't get his claws into it to climb up. I was astonished to see his reaction to this. To this day if he hears children playing, he reacts with joy, but if the child is crying, he gets angry and he shows it. He will finally calm down when the TV is off.

Who do you think acquired the duties of caring for Little Bird? Mom, of course, his enemy.

I kept Little Bird for eighteen years. I had to give him to my real estate friend who had other parrots. Why she changed his name to Freddie, I don't know. Little Bird is very happy there because she has small children that adore him.

By the way, he did learn to say 'Melissa' and 'grandpa' and we are so proud that he did.

DIANA'S DREAM

I had this dream about hands, hands that gave me a strong feeling, full of compassion, non-threatening, total love.

Hands that were lifting me up, supporting me to go through this beautiful maze of color. There were hues of blues, greens, yellows, reds, white, and some black.

As I was dreaming, I felt happy as if these hands were lifting me up and taking me to a new dimension.

There were small hands of children, and hands that looked soft and feminine as women's hands. There were also large rough, yet gentle hands of men.

All these hands were gently pushing me up and helping me go through this tunnel of swirling color. I did not know where these hands were taking me.

Then finally, I could see a mere circle of light at the end of the tunnel, but I still did not know what was there or why I was going there,

While the hands were taking me through, I felt content, joy, and relaxed with a soothing feeling of peace and love.

To this day, years after I had this dream, I still feel the awesomeness of pure love.

TIME (T I M E)

What is meant but the word "Time?" The dictionary describes it as a continuum in which events occur in apparently irreversible succession from the past through the present to the future.

My definition of time is:
> You can't see it!
> You can't taste it!
> You can't feel it!

Time is infinite.

Our first encounter with time begins with our parents. When a woman conceives, a child is created and that is when our clock starts.

We begin life in a time table. First we are children growing up—going to school, and learning what life is all about, and this takes time.

Then time is needed to become an adult. Now, this is where time really comes into play. Time is of the essence:
> Time to go to college
> Time to fall in love
> Time to get married and have a family
> Time for a career
> Time, Time, Time, Time

Time is one of the things we can't control--

And hoping we still have a little time to prepare for our infinite life time.

Our lives are set and only God can end our time.

LOOKING OUT MY KITCHEN WINDOW

I am standing at my kitchen counter having a cup of coffee. I can look out of my window which faces Jackman Street. It is a beautiful sunny morning. I hear the distant sound of bells ringing from Sacred Heart Church. Across the street is a Catholic school, and I am watching the young children who must be in first or second grade coming out to play at recess time.

I start to reminisce of the time I was their age and in school. I remember how I would get excited at recess time. I would hurry to be the first one out the door so that I could get to the tether ball area, because we only had twenty minutes to play and it was first come, first one to play.

My mind continues to wander, and I think about how my mom was able to get me and my sisters into Our Lady Queen of Angels Catholic Grammar School, and how she managed to pay for us because she did not get much money from her monthly county check to support her five daughters and herself. She was a single parent and money was tight.

My mom told me that the school was giving us a break on the tuition and all she had to pay was $3.00 a month for all five of us. My youngest sister, Tio, was in the first grade and I was in the sixth grade. Tuition was only one thing my mom had to figure out, and then there had to be money for uniforms.

As I am leaning on my kitchen counter and writing this, I think about my mom who is now in an assisted living home, my sister Gloria who is also in an assisted living home, and my other sisters who are doing okay. I also think about my baby sister, Lucille, who was lovingly called "Tio." She died some thirty years ago and today is her birthday. She would have been sixty-two years old.

Happy Birthday Tio. I love you and miss you—with tears in my eyes.

ELAINE BROWN

Elaine Brown found her way to the Antelope Valley from her childhood home of Ontario, Canada, where memories of her grandmother reading her children's classics instilled a love of storytelling. She honed her early writing skills by composing letters to friends in distant cities. Later after raising four daughters, she entered the work force as an Executive Assistant, a position that educated her in the short, tight writing requirements of the engineering field

Throughout the years, Elaine's desire to write fiction grew. She took various creative writing courses, but it was her enrollment in an online course with the Long Ridge Writers Group that really pushed her to challenge herself. Now retired, Elaine has more time to devote to writing. She composes short fiction and hopes to branch out into longer efforts. Her co-authors are her ever-present canine desk mates: Mimi, Precious, and Chiqui.

A WIFE'S PREDICAMENT

The homey smell of coffee, bacon and other early morning breakfast smells wafted through the cafe. After two sets of tennis in the warm Miami sun, Angela had proposed that they go to breakfast at the nearby Orange Tree Cafe. With no other plans, Brooke had agreed.

Angela leaned forward as she raised her cup, her face animated from exertion.

"Great game. Perhaps you'll win next time."

"I look forward to the attempt." Brooke's wry tone appeared lost on Angela.

"I'm so glad to have the opportunity to work for an innovative man like your husband. I'm getting such a wonderful education working on research and development at RAD. Peter is so enthusiastic about our new product."

Brooke inwardly grimaced. *Yeah, I'll just bet you'd like to get your pretty little hands on my husband, too. What kind of game are you playing, Angela? What kind of game is Peter playing?*

There was that damning piece of evidence of something amiss when she found a note from Angela to Peter on a bar napkin in his shirt pocket. It had seemed so clandestine and nefarious.

Brooke glanced at Angela, her blond hair swept into a youthful ponytail and sky blue eyes wide-set in a honey-tinted face.

How can I compete with that; I'm at least a decade older than her. I've never been a beauty, but compared to her golden looks I feel like a dull and colorless mess. I can't even control this untidy mass of twisted hair.

She ran unsteady fingers through her own unruly locks and cursed their drab color. She hated the ash shade and dark streaks. Brooke lowered her eyes to Angela's svelte figure and suffered another bout of jealousy.

No wonder I can't seem to win at tennis with her. I probably have an extra twenty pounds to lug around the court.

Trying to make order of her shifting thoughts, Brooke aligned her knife and fork beside her dish. She was confused.

My husband is an FBI agent, and he doesn't have a company called RAD. His work has usually been so straight forward, and mostly in the office at headquarters. What are they up to?

She decided not to tell Angela that her husband was an FBI agent. In fact, she decided not to tell her anything more at all, especially since Angela never seemed to reveal anything about her own life. Instead, she looked into her coffee cup and remembered the day she had met this woman, how Angela had boldly walked up to her at the tennis club and challenged her to a game of tennis. She didn't think anything of it then, but now wondered at the interest Angela had taken in her.

Now, still peering into her coffee, she felt uncomfortable in Angela's presence. Not willing to put it off any longer, she was resolved to ask her about her interest in Peter. She looked up to see Angela's gaze focused beyond Brooke's shoulder.

"You will come with us without making a fuss," said a gruff male voice with a foreign accent. A vice-like grip on Brooke's arm assured her compliance. She started to scream in protest.

"Keep quiet and no one gets hurt!" said the voice, like a line in a bad movie, as he increased the pressure on her arm.

Brooke felt something hard against her shoulder - a gun, perhaps. In a frightening daze, she was led out of the cafe by what she could now see were two burly men.

Her last glimpse of Angela showed an expressionless mask as she remained seated, examining her polished nails.

This can't be happening, thought Brooke. *Why, Angela?* was the betrayal revealed in her shocked eyes.

Unmoved, Angela never looked up.

Brooke's confusion was intensified by this sudden abduction and Angela's lack of concern.

What in hell is going on here? Who are these people? What do they want with me? What does Angela have to do with this?

Her thoughts were interrupted as the two men pushed her into the back seat of a black SUV with dark tinted windows. The man holding the gun got in beside her; the other moved around to the other side and squeezed her between them. She nearly gagged. Both men smelled of heavy garlic and something else Brooke couldn't name.

The driver barreled out of the driveway and headed east. That was the last that Brooke saw before a blindfold was hauled with coarse hands over her eyes. The man yanked her forward and trussed her hands behind her back. In her terror, she tried to bite and kick her assailants. The gun was shoved into her side.

The man growled, "Sit still and be quiet or we will gag you, too. It would be a shame to have to damage such a pretty lady."

"I'd like to do more than rough her up," said the other man. "Too bad we have to deliver her to Vlad in such a hurry. I'd like a piece of this *dziewuszka*."

She heard the leer in his voice and cringed away from the odious man, which brought her painfully closer to the gun in her side.

"What do you want with me?" demanded Brooke. She tried to gulp down her terror. Increased confusion misted her thinking.

"Quiet!" said the man, pushing the gun harder into her side. "Vlad may answer your question if he decides you need to know."

The accent of these men was very heavy. Brooke surmised that they may have been from Eastern Europe, perhaps Russia. She hadn't thought much about it before, but she realized that Angela has a slightly similar accent. Why would they want her? Did it have something to do with Peter's job? Where were they taking her? What would they do to her? These questions crashed in circles around her brain.

Brooke heard the sounds of traffic increase for a while and then dissipate altogether. Was that the salty tang of the ocean? Hard to tell with the stench from the two men.

The car came to a sudden stop. The men pulled Brooke from the SUV and pushed her forward. With the uneven pavement, her hands tied behind her back, and the inability to see, she was afraid she might fall. That would be the least of her problems. Her foot hit a rise in the pavement. She tripped. Both men grabbed her to hold her up and impelled her over some kind of threshold, then through what seemed to be an inner doorway. Rough hands pushed Brooke onto a chair.

"Why are you doing this to me?" Brooke asked, choking back the rusty tang of fear.

"Shut up!" growled the burly man as he tied her to the chair and removed the blindfold.

After the two men left, she inspected the filthy room of the abandoned warehouse. Waves slapped against something outside. Cobwebs clung to everything. She shuddered and wondered where the spiders were. Clutter littered the floor. She sneezed. And just as she began to examine and discard all the reasons why she might be in this position, another man came in and stood before her. Short and arrogant, with feet spread wide he glared down at her.

"Who are you, and what do you want with me?" Brooke whispered.

Ignoring her questions, the man said, "Perhaps with you as incentive, your husband will give us what we want." He pulled out a cell phone and punched in some numbers. "Mr. Logan, we have your wife. In exchange for her freedom, we want the prototype of your new invention and the specifications for the new bullet propellant."

The man listened briefly, and then pushed the phone toward her. "Tell your husband you are okay."

"Peter, what's going on? Who are these peop...?" Brooke cried into the phone before the man jerked it away.

"I'll call again with instructions about where to deliver the prototype and specs," said the man before he ended the call and stalked out of the room.

Although the day had become hot, Brooke shivered in cold shock. *I need to calm myself and think of how to get out of here*, she thought.

113

She dragged herself and the chair toward a dust-covered desk. With her back toward it, she managed to pull out the center drawer. She found nothing useful - pens, ruler, the usual office supplies. As she was about to give up, her fingers found the shape of scissors.

It took time, effort, and a painful cut to her wrist, but she eventually freed herself from the ropes. In the corner, she saw a large tarp. She lifted it with shaking fingers. Among several small tools, she found a length of pipe.

The men who put me here were careless, and not too smart, thought Brooke. She felt a little more confident. But further searching showed no way out.

She grabbed the pipe, dragged the chair back to where she had first been placed, wrapped the ropes around her feet and hands, and waited. She was barely in place when Angela sauntered in.

"What's going on, Angela?" Her eyes pleaded for answers. "How are you involved in this kidnapping?"

"I've been working with Peter Logan, your devoted husband, trying to get information and access to a prototype of his new invention." Angela pushed a stray lock of her hair back into her ponytail. "It is a small, long-range weapon with lock-on target capability, and it uses a new powerful propellant. It will be most useful to our client. But, I'm sure he's shared some of this information with you." Angela continued, her eyes hardening. "You're the bait to get his compliance to our demand."

She waved a gun in Brooke's face several times as she paced before her. Then Angela noticed the disturbed dust on the desk, and went over to inspect it.

Swift and sure, Brooke moved toward Angela's back. With mighty force, she brought the pipe down on Angela's head. Angela sprawled unconscious on the floor. Brooke seized the gun. She had barely enough time to hide behind a cabinet before the man with the phone came in.

He looked around, astonished to see Angela on the floor and no one in the chair. He reached for his gun. Not waiting, Brooke pulled the trigger. She sent a thankful prayer for the target practices Peter had insisted upon. The man fell. Blood streamed from the hole in his chest. Shocked eyes stared at her as he lost consciousness.

Brooke could hear gunshots from outside the door. The gun still in her hand, she nearly fainted as Peter burst through the door.

"Brooke! Are you okay?" shouted Peter. Professional calm failed him. He took the gun from her and wrapped his arms around her quaking body.

John Foster's office seemed too small to encase the massive, powerful man who sat behind the desk. As though from a distance, Brooke heard John, Peter's handler, say that Vlad was dead, and Angela was brain dead from the head trauma.

"Brooke, you are very pale," said Peter. "Can you continue?"

A weak "Yes" was all she could summon for the moment.

"You were so brave, Brooke," said Peter grasping her cold hand.

She turned abruptly to Peter and asked, "Why did Angela think you owned a business?"

"We've been trying to bring down Vlad's illegal weapons dealing here in Miami," said John. He leaned toward her. "You've done the job for us, Mrs. Logan. Thank you."

"I'm sorry you became involved," added John. "Vlad, Angela, and their thugs did their homework well before approaching Peter. We had them under surveillance from the beginning. However, our job continues as the Russian mob will find replacements for them."

"I did nothing but try to stay alive," cried Brooke wrenching her hand from Peter's. "How could you let them kidnap me? I was terrified."

She stood and turned angry eyes on him. "We have a lot to talk about when we get home."

JOURNEY THROUGH AUTUMN

The year was 1946, and I was seven years old and full of curiosity. The heat and humidity of summer had gradually given way to the brisk dry air of autumn in this city of Windsor deep at the bottom of the province of Ontario, Canada.

I kicked up leaves that scurried in my path as I walked to school. Leaves bounced and whisked by, pushed along by the breeze. My imagination had them hurrying in the wake of the Mad Hatter on his way to that most important meeting.

I stopped now and then to pick up a particularly colorful maple leaf and admire its different vibrant hues. It would have to wait until my return home from school for me to collect it, along with the most beautiful specimens of the leaves. I continued on to shuffle through the leaves in my path, and those in the air, some of which caught in my hair until I reached my school.

My return home was not much different from my trip there in the cool morning. However, the air was much warmer and the breeze had slowed to a crawl. I had been told we were in an "Indian Summer" weather condition where the warmth of summer returned again for a few days almost as a gift before the cold weather set in.

It was almost overwhelming, the number of beautiful red and gold maple leaves that covered my path. I bent often to pick up and examine the leaves. Some were almost all vermillion, scarlet and maroon. Some were mixed vermillion and pink with touches of green and yellow. Some were all yellow, and some were still green. I gathered a mix of colors and piled them carefully on top of each other.

Upon arriving home, I placed them on the kitchen table in preparation of the task of preserving them. There on the table were three apple pies whose aroma scented the house with a hint of cinnamon. Heat wafted up from the center of them, so I knew that they had just been removed from the oven. My mouth watered and I could hardly wait for supper to be over to sample a piece of one of those delicious smelling pies.

While supper was being prepared, I headed back outside and grabbed a rake. My friend Patsy came by with her rake, and we made piles of leaves in the middle of the front yard. We rolled and played in the leaves laughing in glee as we tossed handfuls into the air.

I was aware of how the dry leaves crackled and split apart, and how their powdered dryness filled my nostrils with a stifling pungent scent.

Soon it was time for dinner. I bid Patsy farewell as I ran to the back door. My hair and clothing were full of the dry leaves which I brushed off before entering the house. I washed my hands and hurried to set the table.

I was hungry from all my play, but still could hardly wait to eat my share of the apple pie. All through supper, I thought about when my grandparents and I had gone to the apple orchard in the country to pick up apples from the ground below the trees. I spent my time in the trees climbing and eating apples. I loved the sweet tart fragrance of the orchard, and was sorry to have to leave it.

Finally, I got to eat some of the pie and was not disappointed. After supper, I helped dry the dishes. Then it was time to work on the beautiful leaves I had collected. Grannie got out the iron and waxed paper. We proceeded to put the leaves between pieces of waxed paper and then iron them. Now I had my colorful leaves preserved in wax so that I could admire them for many days to come.

The next day was just as lovely as the day before with many more leaves falling from the trees and littering the ground. That evening after supper, Grannie brought out a good sized pumpkin and proceeded to cut the top off, and then cut a face with a toothy smile into the side of it. She called it a jack-o-lantern. We waited until the next night to put the jack-o-lantern outside with a candle inside of it. I was intrigued by how the flickering candle made ghoulish shadows on its face. That evening I dressed as a witch and hoped that I would scare people into putting candy in my basket. Of course, I came home with lots of candies and even apples and some coins. I felt life was wonderful.

The next morning, I woke to notice a visit from Jack Frost who had breathed his icy patterns upon my windows. Through the clearer spaces on the window, I could see that the trees in the park and on the street were almost bare of leaves. Even the ground looked a bit white with hoar frost. My room was chilly as I hastened to put on my robe and slippers before heading down stairs for breakfast.

Even though autumn had been vibrant with color and beauty, Jack Frost promised a beauty of his own.

DENISE DALO-SCHIPPER

Denise Dalo-Schipper was born in Los Angeles, California. Growing up primarily in Southern California, she was fortunate to experience life in various places in the United States. She is the daughter of an architect/contractor father and an attorney mother. Her educational background consists of a Bachelor's degree in Liberal Studies with a Teaching Credential from California State University (CSU) Northridge, and a Master's degree in Curriculum and Instruction from CSU Bakersfield. She is retired from 20+ years of teaching kindergarten.

Denise has always loved to read and write, and in her retirement is enjoying writing fiction stories. She believes that life is a gift, and she loves to read and share stories of the blessings, drama, and silliness that life has to offer.

Currently a resident of Southern California, Denise is married and the mother of two wonderful teenage boys, with whom she shares stories, travels, and just plain fun.

A PLACE FOR MOM

The night began like any other. My teenage boys were in bed, and all was right with the world. Or so we thought. Little did we know that just less than two miles away was something that would change our lives dramatically.

We have all heard the Life Alert ad: "I've fallen and I can't get up!" For the past year I have been strongly suggesting that Jan, my 79 year old mother-in-law, get one, as she was getting unsteady on her feet and lived alone in a senior apartment. She finally agreed, but it was too late to help her.

On the night I spoke of, she wished she had Life Alert. She called my husband Rick at about 2:30 in the morning. She had fallen around 8:30 that night and could not get up for about six and a half hours. When she was finally able to grab a lamp to knock the phone down off the counter, the first thing she said after finally getting a hold of Rick was, "Denise was right."

I was glad she called Rick, but I couldn't help but wonder why she didn't call 911 instead of her son. At any rate, Rick rushed to her place and brought our barely adult son, Tyler. Between the two of them they got her up and to the emergency room at the local hospital.

Jan had been having more pain than usual, just two days after Rick returned from his vacation in Bishop, he took her to her doctor. She sat there so long that he finally just took her home at her insistence since she was in more pain. They had been at the medical facility for over four hours with many tests but no help. She already has back and hip joint problems as well as leg weakness and pain. One of her legs has a problem, and she has been using a walker whenever we have gone places for at least six months.

The next few days she was in a tremendous amount of pain. All they did was test after test for a variety of problems that seemed to have little to do with her hip, back, and leg pain. The pain continued with no abatement for several days until the night that everything changed.

Can you believe the hospital sent her home to her apartment with a broken ankle? With her pain and weakness in one leg, and the broken ankle on the other leg she was unable to get up to even take care of personal business.

Rick and Tyler spent the next few days and nights at Jan's apartment getting little sleep, just to help her get to and from the portable potty chair. There wasn't even a place for them to both sleep at the same time, and Jan got up every 2-3 hours. They had to support her full weight of 140 pounds when they lifted her. It was killing Rick's back. I felt that this couldn't go on. We needed help. Things had to change! Jan's insurance would not provide aides to help her at home. We needed to get her into some sort of convalescent place.

After some deliberations Rick, with help from Tyler, took Jan back to the emergency room. After many hours they did admit her to a health care convalescent center. While she was there, the medical facility started to create reasons why they thought she should go home. Thank goodness the Medicare advocates helped her stay until she got her cast off and could walk a bit.

I first discussed making a place for his mom at our house when Rick was adamant that Jan would absolutely not be willing to move here. He maintained that she only planned on returning to her apartment. I believed her moving in to our home was the only thing that made sense. Rick and Tyler could not continue to stay at Jan's, and Jan could not continue living alone. She could very well have another fall. She was so fearful of having one that she was unable to even try to walk at that point.

My mother-in-law and I weren't that close then, but I knew she was a good person. Not to mention the huge fact that she saved my youngest son's life when he was maybe two years old and was hanging by a foot and a hand outside of a balcony on a fifth story apartment! She more than earned my gratitude that day!

I wanted very much to help her. She is my husband's mother, and my children's grandmother. I knew that I could not help her due to my own health issues but I wanted to do what I could, and give her the quality of life she deserves. With a few alterations to our house we could have her move in to our downstairs office, soon to be bedroom.

Unfortunately, I made the mistake of planning her move and asking friends at church to set up some teens and young adults to help. They would move Jan's furniture to our house. I also talked with a gentleman at our church who is a contractor, as we also needed to add doors to the office, and a shower to the downstairs bathroom.

You might say I jumped the gun! Rick does not deal well with change, and he doesn't like to ask people for help. I should have remembered that. I can and do respect that; I should have thought things out further.

Rick was very upset and verbally harassed me on the ride from church to home. He was steadfast that Jan would never agree. I complied and quickly put the idea on a back burner. I still knew in my heart that she would not be able to live alone any longer, but tried to let things play out as they might.

Sandy, my sister-in-law who lives in Arkansas, also kindly offered to have Jan move in with them. They have plenty of room for her; however, Jan wanted to remain in California.

Funny, when we bought our house I wanted to change the downstairs office into a bedroom at some point. I knew it would be a necessity eventually, when Rick and I were older and unable to climb the stairs.

I thought about how in different times and cultures that people lived in multi-generational homes with grandparents, parents, children, and sometimes aunts or uncles, too. You don't hear about that happening as much in this generation. Even my hairdresser was firm in telling me that it would never happen for her; that is, her mother-in-law was never moving in to live with them. She thought I was a saint.

I am not a saint, but am just thinking ahead for all of my family. Why was I so willing to do this? I thought back to my mother. When I was 20 years old, my mother became ill and was in the hospital for more than three weeks. Although she had heart attacks, she planned on coming home. We all did. She wanted me to quit my job to take care of her. I wasn't thrilled with the idea, as I liked my freedom and had supported myself for four years. Her doctors met with me and told me that her heart muscle had been 75% damaged, and another heart attack would kill her.

Her hopes and mine didn't work out, and she had her final heart attack and passed. I wasn't able to help her, but I could help Jan. She deserves it.

So a few days after Rick told me to scrub the plans, guess what happened? He told me that Jan realized that she could not live alone any longer. When Rick told her that I had already been planning the move and construction, she was extremely surprised and pleased. She said, "I didn't know I was wanted." I was really glad that Rick told her all the plans I had made for her benefit and of my love for her.

We had about three weeks to move her furniture out of her senior apartment and hoped for a bit longer to get the construction completed. So began a huge flurry of activity - Rick packing up her apartment, getting quotes, finding out if there was a shower drain under the cabinets to no avail. We added doors, and hired a contractor to do the installation and redo the tile floor in the bathroom. We finally got everything ready.

It was up to the doctors and convalescent place to get Jan ready. Unfortunately, she was on a lot of medication. They could only give pain medicine when requested, and not on any type of schedule.

As a result, the doctor kept increasing her meds. She was not herself. She was depressed, despondent, and unable to help herself.

We were worried that she would not be able to help herself in any way to get up and down. She couldn't seem to do the physical therapy as her mind told her she wasn't supposed to bear any weight on her one leg, and couldn't put any weight on the leg with the ankle cast. When she had the cast removed, after about a week of physical therapy, the time came for her to move out and go to our home.

It was a Sunday, and we went to church in the morning as usual. At around 2 p.m. that afternoon the transportation van brought her home. We had shown her pictures of the new room, and had worked to organize her furniture. We had much of her belongings still in boxes for her to help sort. The day before she came, my youngest son Jacob helped me dust, vacuum and clean her room so it would be ready for her. We had the portable potty chair ready, her favorite chair that would practically stand her up, and the television was up and running. At Rick's request, I had even made a sign for her door that said, "A Place for Mom."

We worked hard to get all this ready, but were worried about whether it would work out. I personally believed that it would, and prayed often, too. This is what families are for, in my opinion. We made a special invitation to her to welcome her into our home. I had a good feeling that it would work out well. And it did. Our life was definitely changed and for the better!

JACKIE L. CROSSWHITE SR.

Jackie Crosswhite spent most of his life in Southern California. He now resides in Lancaster, California, and loves the high desert climate and the open country where there are not so many people.

He originally hails from the Country and Western music state of Mississippi, where he began writing songs at the early age of twelve. His dream then was to become a professional song writer. He is now enjoying writing as a member of the Antelope Valley Writers Association. This is the third anthology in which his writings have been published. In addition to writing songs, he is working on a book of his memoirs, a book of short stories, and a novel.

WHO ME

Who am I to-day

I'm no-body in par-ticu-lar

Just me and that's all.

I.D.

One, two, three, four, five

Is that my age or I.Q.

I don't know for sure.

LITTLE JACK
(Song Lyric)

Let me tell you about a man named Jack.
That's me, Little Jack, and that's a fact.
I'm bad as lighting, and mean as thunder.
Mess with me. I'll put you six feet under.
If you don't want a monkey on your back,
don't mess around with Little Jack.

I was born on Friday, a full moon night,
A stormy 13th, and I'm in the devil's sight.
My dad fed me beer before I could walk.
He had me fighting before I could talk.
If you don't want a monkey on your back,
don't mess around with Little Jack.

He took his dog and hid, this Mr. Brown,
when he heard that Little Jack was in town.
I beat up Big John and stomped Big Percy.
If I get on to you, you'll beg for mercy.
If you don't want a monkey on your back,
don't mess around with Little Jack.

Mr. Big Foot and I had a heck of a fight.
He took off and disappeared into the night.
He's still running, and he hasn't been back.
He don't want anything from Little Jack.
If you don't want a monkey on your back,
don't mess around with Little Jack.

I've fought with bears and wrestled gators.
And if I had to, I'd take on the Terminator.
You want-to-be-bad boys, wherever you're at,
Around the corner is another Little Jack.
If you don't want a monkey on your back,
don't mess around with Little Jack.

FADING MARRIAGE
(Song Lyric)

Oh baby, baby, we need to fix our marriage.
It's tearing us apart.
Slowly and surely, it's fading away from
what it was at the start.

For the sake of our family, we can make it
work if we really want to.
All that we have to do is to do
all that we have to do.

Remember, we were sweethearts through high
school and college. Then we settled down,
We got married , had our children, and we
bought our home just outside of town.

Everything went great for a few years.
Then, it began going downhill slowly.
And, if we don't get back to our real world
our marriage will be lost. For surely

We've come too far to give up now.
Let's get our lives back together.
If we get out of our worlds and meet in
the middle, our marriage will be better.

For the sake of our family we can make it
work if we really want to.
All that we have to do is to do
all that we have to do.

IT MEANT EVERYTHING
(Song Lyric)

Hear the sleigh bells ring,
Hear the children sing,
It's Christmas time in L.A.

Though it doesn't snow
All the children know
Santa Clause is on his way.

If you've been really good
Like you know you should
All good gifts will come to you.

That's what life's about.
It's time to figure out
It's what you do that paves the way.

How long have you lived for,
Just how long did you believe
When you were that child expecting Santa?
It meant everything.

Candles burn bright
Into the Christmas night.
As the flames burn,
Love fills the air.

Smile and spread good cheer
Today and through the year.
Christmas is a holiday.

MY SIXTH GRADE FAN CLUB

Yes, I have a fan club. I am a writer, and I have a fan club made up of elementary school students.

On May 15, 2015, I picked up my granddaughter, Jessica, from Sunnydale Elementary School. On our way back to the car, we were approached by five of her eleven year old classmates. Two of them are brother and sister. One other boy I knew, and two of them I didn't know. The brother asked me if I was a writer. I said yes, and asked him why he asked?

He said that my granddaughter told them that I was a writer. They were interested in writing and asked for help. They wanted to know if I had some books in print, and if I would give them one to read. I said I didn't have a book ready to print, but that I'm working on three.

I told them, "I do have published works in two of my writing group's anthologies, and I will give you one of each."

I asked them to promise me that they would take care of the books. They promised. I autographed the two anthologies, and I gave them some other books that I had. They really enjoyed them.

Jessica and her friends are all in the top of their class in reading. Two of Jessica's neighbors are also interested in writing. They asked me for help, too.

Hey, future writers of the Antelope Valley Writers Association, have confidence in yourself, and you can do it. Don't let anyone take your dreams from you. Writing something is easy; getting it published is the hard part. When you think of something to write, put it on paper. It's such a great feeling, writing down words that people enjoy reading. You can even get it published and get it on the market, and maybe even make some money. There's money to be made out there, if that is your goal, and by good writers like you. All that it will cost to start is a pencil and a sheet of paper.

JAMES F. WOOD

Jim Wood was born in Massachusetts in a house on a hill overlooking the Boston Navy Yard. He now lives in Palmdale, California, and is a forty-five year resident of the Antelope Valley.

His first poem bubbled to the surface of his mind when he was in the fifth grade. He believes a higher power unlocked the talent in him to help him begin, at last, to get over being orphaned five years earlier. In junior high, the teachers were trying to figure out how in the world he was ever going to support himself as an adult, if his aunt didn't agree to put him in a Special Education class. Some of his classmates there paid him a quarter a piece to do their homework whenever writing a poem was the assignment.

More years than he cares to remember have passed since then. He got married, had children, and worked in the aircraft industry for what seemed like a lifetime. And here he is, an old guy, writing poetry on a machine he never dreamed could exist way back in the 1940s and 50s.

TURNING POINT

I'm told I ought to live in the present,

See, hear, do,

Pack new adventure into each passing moment.

But it's autumn and the air is golden.

Ripened fruit hangs heavy.

Leaves are falling.

As each shortened day grows colder,

I remember green, growing spring,

The warm days of summer.

OCTOBER VIEW
(From Red Rock)

The air was sharp. The sun was bright.

Its light, reflected in each wavelet,

Was fluid art, regulated with care

Or abandon by wind and currents.

Like us, that sea was born one drop at a time

Had fallen as rain that nourished the earth

Tore out gullies, great canyons;

And every drop of it

Had returned from where it came, again and again.

That day the waves touched the rock gently

Like the gull's shadows that slid across the red stone,

And the sea sound spoke to me,

But I cannot tell you what it said.

There are no words.

LETTERS FROM AMY

The first thing Hal Guthrie did when he was discharged from the Air Force was to go see Amy Johnson. He'd only met Amy once, when he was home on leave the year before. He'd asked her to write to him because he was going overseas. Since then he'd received two letters every month. They were nice letters, each a little more personal than the last. It was because of the letters that he'd fallen in love with Amy. Now he was going to her apartment to tell her so.

He rang the doorbell to her apartment, and a little brunette answered. "Is Amy in? I'm Hal Guthrie," he explained.

"She moved about a month ago," the girl said. "I'm Paula Fuller. We were roommates."

"Do you know where?" Hal asked.

Paula shook her head. "No, she didn't leave any forwarding address."

When Hal turned to go she said, "Wait." He turned back to her. "Look," she said. "You're not going to be able to find her on Sunday. Why don't we get some sandwiches and beer from the delicatessen and have a picnic on Moccasin Hill? I hate to see you waste your first day back."

Hal wouldn't have been tempted but Moccasin Hill held memories. He'd played there as a child. "It might be fun," he said.

They set up their blanket on the side of the hill so they had a sweeping country view. "I used to dig for arrowheads up here when I was a kid," Hal said.

"I was a sandbox specialist myself." Paula dug in the portable icebox for sandwiches. "I came up here quite a bit though."

Hal laughed. "You know, in her letters Amy said she used to play up here, too."

It turned out to be a wonderful afternoon. They spent it charting out the changes that had taken place around the hill since they were children and watching the gangs of kids that roved over the hill. There was a sturdy band of pioneers tracking long-dead Indians. A gang of cutthroats passed by in search of Captain Kidd's treasure, and although their costumes weren't eighteenth-century, their language was spicy enough to be authentic.

"They ought to have their mouths washed out with soap," Paula said.

Hal laughed. "Whoever heard of a pirate that didn't swear a little?"

Hal took Paula home about six o'clock. He carried her icebox up to her apartment for her. "Thanks for the afternoon, Paula," he said.

"I had a wonderful time," Paula walked him to the door. "If you don't find Amy, give me a call."

Hal nodded just to be polite. He was sure that in all those letters he'd find something that would lead him to Amy.

That night Hal sat up late and reread Amy's letters. He found the name of the place where she worked right off, but it wasn't until later that he found any reference to the street it was on.

The next morning he got up around ten and went down there. The girl at the desk frowned.

"Amy Johnson? No, I can't think of anyone working here by that name, but if you wait a minute I'll check the records." She went down the hall to another office. A few moments later she was back with a folder in her hand. "She quit about eight months ago," the girl said.

"Quit?" Hal echoed.

"To get married," the girl explained.

The words struck Hal like a thunderbolt. He couldn't believe it. He wandered off towards the door to the street. He was standing there just outside the door when the eleven o'clock shift let out and the street started filling up with people going to lunch.

"Well, hi." It was Paula. The two girls who came out with her went the other way. "What are you doing down here?"

"I was looking for Amy, but she quit eight months ago." Hal walked up the street with her. "Don't tell me you work at Grammet's, too."

She nodded. "For almost two years now."

They turned into a restaurant and found a booth. Hal waited until the waitress had taken their order and gone, before he asked Paula, "Is Amy really married?"

Paula fiddled with the salt shaker a moment before saying, "Look, didn't you think it was a little strange yesterday that I should suggest a picnic on Moccasin Hill of all places?"

"Yes, but..." Hal started.

"How do you think I knew it was your first day back?" Paula continued.

131

The waitress brought their order. Hal just sat there with his mouth open.

"Then you've been the one who's been writing to me, using her name?"

Paula nodded, "Yes."

"What was the matter with your own name? Were you ashamed of it?" Hal felt she'd made a fool of him, and he was angry.

Paula looked around to see if anyone was staring at them. "No," she said in a low voice. "When you met Amy, she was already engaged. She couldn't write to you. I thought you'd like to get letters from somebody you'd at least met than from a complete stranger.

"So you sent me up in a nice little *papier-mâché* space capsule and put me into orbit." Hal's voice was louder and a few people at the counter were beginning to turn. "That's real nice. The only trouble is like now...re-entry."

"All I did was sign Amy's name. You act like I committed a crime or something," Paula whispered as if to compensate for Hal's shouting.

Hal got to his feet and stomped out. He was halfway up the street before he'd calmed down a little and remembered the bill. He hurried back just in time to see Paula going into the Grammet building.

That night he thought about burning the letters, but he didn't. Instead, he threw them into the bottom draw of his desk and went to a movie. It was a love story and every time it got a little sentimental, Hal thought of the letters and Paula. By the time he got home from the movie, he decided he would read the letters, once more, just to see how many lies he could detect in them.

Reading the letters wasn't a good idea. The longer he read them, the more he came to realize that there really weren't any lies in them, and that he wasn't in love with Amy at all but with the girl who wrote the letters, Paula.

He called her up the next evening after she got home from work.

"What do you want?" Paula asked.

"Look, Paula," Hal said. "I'm sorry about yesterday. I don't blame you for being mad."

"Well, I'm mad all right," she agreed, but her voice had a doubtful quality to it, as if she was waiting to be convinced.

"I thought we might go out to dinner," Hal said.

"Going out to dinner with you costs too much!"

The way she'd snapped the sentence out Hal thought she'd hung up. He was still standing there with the phone to his ear when she said, "Are you still there?"

"I sure am," he answered. "How about dinner tonight? It won't cost you a cent and it will give me a chance to tell you how much I love you."

"Well, I guess an awful lot of the trouble was my fault," she said. "Give me an hour to get dressed."

Hal hung up the phone smiling. It was good to be home.

PASSING OF A QUIET MEADOW

Our meadow is gone.
While we grew old the forest
Crept down from the hill
And conquered it.

The young wood is dark
Crowded with nodding giants.
It smells of cedar, pine, hemlock.
I walk among tall trees and
Scraps of spangled sunlight.
Once deer grazed here.

You and I
Lay in the tall yellow grass
Watched red tailed hawks
Floating on the blue air
High above us.

When storm clouds crested
The wooded hill
We raced each other home
Arriving in a gale of laughter
Not always before the rain.

ZORRO AND THE LONE RANGER
(In loving memory)

Imagining
I was Zorro or the Lone Ranger
I sent my queen unprotected
or guarded only by a knight
out to face impossible odds.

I lived on dreams of the oooh's and aaah's
when through some brilliant
completely unorthodox move
I won the game.
Those moves, if ever, seldom came.
Usually it was tough luck Jim
looking surprised when his hammer
came down on an empty chamber

It taught me about dreams.
In time they become narrow specters
that cling like lovers wanting kisses,
whispering from hollow hearts
promises that won't be kept.

So I bid *Adios*, to *Mi amigos*,
Zorro, the Lone Ranger.
Now I let the game unfold,
moving pawns, bishops, rooks, and queen
each at its required time.

I've become dull predictable establishment,
leading a posse when I ride out.
I win, but my conscience tortures me.
Zorro and the Lone Ranger were buried alive.

ENCOUNTER WITH A CLAY PROPHET

I met a strange ragged old man.

His beard was stained nicotine yellow.

His eyes were a watery blue.

"For the price of a cup of coffee," he said,

"I'll give eternal life to you."

"Get real," I said, but waited.

He said, "There is no life, only living.

There is no death, only dying.

And to puzzle you more there's a paradox."

He stopped for effect or to study my face.

Then he smiled.

"You cannot live until you die,

To self," he added wryly.

"Who do I love but me?" I snapped.

"You love your fellow men," he said.

"Why should I not indulge myself?"

"Indulge your neighbors first," said he.

"And not be scared, if something is going down?"

He raised his hands, and arms outspread

"Trust in me. Have faith," he said.

I peeled a fiver off my roll.

The deepening dusk could not hide his joy.

He tottered down the street and stopped

Beneath a neon liquor sign.

"God bless you," he said, and went inside.

LOIS WILK

Lois Wilk arrived in the Antelope Valley in 1956 where she was a stay-at-home wife and mother. In the 1970s she was asked to work for her local church as the parish caller, a position where she had the opportunity to meet many people.

During this time she was approached by a local travel agency to assist in putting together groups interested in cruises. Never thinking this would be a complete change in her life, she started taking groups on cruises to exotic destinations.

Eventually, Lois opened her own agency (Odyssey Cruises) which she ran for fourteen years before returning to the original agency where she began. She continued there until her retirement.

With a wealth of stories from her world travels, Lois was encouraged to write a book about her experiences during the thirty-five years of traveling to 108 countries. Her book of adventures, *All Aboard...Let's Sail*, will be coming out soon.

ALLIGATOR HUNT

We arrived at LAX to find our terminal empty! I was taking a group on a 21-day trip. It was seven nights sailing the Amazon River and fourteen days cruising southward and ending in Buenos Aires, Argentina.

Going up to the counter, an agent stated, "The airline is going on strike at midnight and a lot of people have cancelled or left earlier in the day."

Fortunately for us we were heading for Miami to connect with another plane flying us to Manaus, Brazil, where we would embark on our cruise. The flights were through the cruise line, so it was their responsibility to get us to the port.

Our plane took off on time and we arrived in Miami around dinner time. Checking in with the cruise line, we were told our flight would be later than our original departure time. After getting something to eat, we returned to the passenger area and waited.

While sitting there we could see the president of the cruise line running around trying to get us a plane and crew before midnight when the strike would begin. He found a flight crew who accepted his proposition. If they took us, his clients, they would receive a free cruise from the line. We took off right before midnight as the airline strike began. Arriving the next day in Manaus, several hours late, we were transferred to the ship.

It was late afternoon when we arrived. We had an early dinner, as we had plans to go on an alligator hunt on the Amazon River.

A ship about the size of a ferry boat transferred us to another dock in the dark of night. We could see lights and small boats docked with men standing around waiting for us to arrive. We disembarked the large ship and were directed to the small putt-putt boats. Our boat held a total of eight. There were two rows of three passengers, our guide in the front of the boat looking for alligators, and a boy bringing up the rear and guiding the motor.

We traveled out into the darkness. I was sitting on the edge and all I could think of was an alligator leaping out of the water and grabbing me. We were only inches from the surface!

To find alligators, a bright spotlight is placed on the front of the boat and turned back and forth. When the guide sees red eyes, he has found an alligator. Every time we got close, the alligator would slide into the water and disappear.

Finally we caught a baby alligator about five feet long. The guide pulled it into our boat and we all had an opportunity to touch his belly. The alligators become docile when being rubbed lying on their backs. Placing him back in the water, the guide instructed the boy to start the motor. Nothing happened.

Ye, gods, are we going to be stuck out here in unknown territory in the darkness? It seems the blades on the motor got clogged with reeds and it couldn't connect. The boy stepped in the water and undid the tangled mess. I was worried about him and hoped that nothing bad would happen.

Traveling back through the darkness listening to the sounds of the jungle and the motor was soothing and a relief as we headed for the ship and civilization. It was a great day to begin our adventures in South America.

HERNANDO'S HIDEAWAY

Each time I repeat a port visit, I try to take a different shore excursion. This time we had the whole day, from 9 a.m. till midnight, to spend in Juneau, Alaska. I decided to take the helicopter ride out to Mendenhall Glacier.

When we reached shore, we were loaded on an old school bus and headed out to the tiny airport. Once there, we were given boots and rain coats. Meanwhile, a girl asked our weights so they could balance the helicopter, and she arranged us so that one person sat in front with the pilot, and three were jammed in back. Fortunately, I got an outside window, so I was able to take in the incredible view flying over the city and up to the glacier.

I took my camera to take a photo, but all I could see in the viewfinder was white. Thinking something must be wrong, I took the camera away from my eyes only to discover that it really was white everywhere. The snow-covered valley fell away as we approached the landing area atop the massive glacier.

Glaciers can be terrifying. After we landed, the guide showed us the deep, sparkling blue crevasses to avoid. If you fell in, they might not be able to rescue you. I was too frightened to get close to the edges, so I wandered among the eerily beautiful and stark ice field until it was time to go.

When we returned to the airport in Juneau and shed our coats and boots, the tour company fortified us with hot chocolate and coffee before taking us back to town. We re-boarded the ship just in time for a pleasant lunch in the dining room. At this time, open seating was just beginning to be offered as an option. With open seating, you choose any seat you like, at any time during the lunch hours. When we chose a different table from the one that had been assigned to us for dinner, our Italian waiter and busboy were beside themselves, and insisted that they would wait on us even if we were at the "wrong" table.

Returning to town after lunch, I went shopping with one of the girls we were traveling with. I was determined to find a Christmas ornament to add to my collection from all over the world, in a store I had spotted earlier. Once there, talking with the owner, I learned that one of my old friends from my hometown was living there in Juneau with her husband. Small world!

At dinner that night, our waiter and busboy invited the three of us ladies to go out dancing, so at 10 p.m. we met them on the pier. We walked together up the several blocks back to the same building where we had shopped earlier in the day. The owner of the shop waved a cheery "hello" as we walked back to the elevator.

The elevator door opened, and I screamed, "HOLY COW!" It was Hernando's Hideaway. My mouth dropped open. There were hundreds of people. Ahead of us was the enormous bar. On the left were tables and chairs crammed with customers. On the right was a half-acre of dance floor with music blasting, and people dancing, and music videos projected onto a huge screen.

The busboy produced a crisp $100 bill and bought us all the first round. The waiter took turns dancing with all three of us, and the busboy began a fruitless flirtation with the youngest lady.

I spotted the girl from the helicopter ride standing alone, so we included her with us and enjoyed learning more about her. She was a college student from Oregon, and this was her summer job that was to pay for her next school year.

That bar must have been the only entertainment around. It was jammed with locals, Indians, Eskimos, crews from two ships plus passengers, and lots of young college students, all dancing and having a great time.

A midnight departure often results in the gangplank being pulled about a half hour before. I glanced at the time - 11:30 already! We hightailed it out of there back to the ship, abandoning the waiter and busboy at the bar, and arriving just before the gangplank was lifted back to the ship. Another close call and another memorable evening!

HANDKERCHIEFS

My sister called to read me an article from her local newspaper about handkerchiefs. Handkerchiefs were used by everyone years ago. There was no Kleenex at that time. Dainty handkerchiefs were carried when socializing in public. Otherwise, a regular hanky was usually plain and a bit larger than the dainty. Men always had large, white, square handkerchiefs for work. At social gatherings they had handkerchiefs with monogram initials placed on them. Then a small, colorful, square hanky was placed in a man's suit jacket.

My mother's side of the family always used hankies, so I grew up with the same habit. A hankie is always with me. Yes, I do use Kleenex when I have a cold or illness. My hankies are just there for me.

I have brought some different hankies from near and far. Every time I went to Spain or Portugal I couldn't resist buying some more. I also have handkerchiefs from the Canary Islands, China, Venice, Italy, and Japan. I haven't used them because though beautiful, they are all white. If I place one of these in my purse alongside a Kleenex, I can't find them, as they don't show up against the tissue.

I have a western hankie that I used at fair time. My daughter thought she was buying me blue-colored hankies but they turned out to be napkins.

Once I was desperate. A friend invited me to her mother's home after her death to see if there was anything I wanted to buy. While going through the house, my friend pulled out some handkerchiefs. I was ecstatic as she gave me all five of them. They were colored. I was very happy for a few years until they started to get thin and ragged. I finally had to discard them. Again, no more colored handkerchiefs.

My family would ask, "What do you want for your birthday or Christmas or Mother's Day?"

I wanted colored handkerchiefs. They never could find any. We have all looked at Target, 99 cent store, Wal-Mart, drug stores, and every department store. I guess no one buys them anymore.

Somehow I am on a catalog list as each week I receive at least five different catalogs. They can be selling clothes, shoes, linens, health food, and all sorts of things.

One day roaming through a catalog I was struck dumb! Here were colorful handkerchiefs for sale. I was ecstatic. I quickly got out my credit card and called the 800 number and ordered twelve colorful hankies. I was so happy when they arrived.

These hankies should last me until my final time on earth. If there are still new ones remaining, I hope my kids will give them to someone who appreciates having colorful handkerchiefs.

LORETTA J. JONES

Loretta Jones was born and raised in Texas and has been writing fiction stories since 1979. Her interest in writing first stemmed from reading "True Detective" stories as a child.

She moved to Los Angeles in 1980 to work in the film industry. She worked for two film-financing companies, one in Beverly Hills and the other was at the old Francis Ford Coppola film studios. She answered phones, read scripts, and made suggestions for casting the actors for roles in films. Later she worked for a film distributing company in acquisitions. Her job was to find independent films for the company and get the films' American and foreign distribution rights. Loretta was also an actress, guest starring in TV and films. Another of her many talents was working as a hairstylist, make-up artist, and special effects make-up artist for commercials, TV and films.

THE UNSOLVED MYSTERIES OF SYLVIA

I think sometimes certain people are brought into our lives under strange circumstances, beyond our conscious level of knowledge. Wayne was one of these strange unusual consequences in my life.

Wayne was a tall, handsome young model. Eventually Wayne opened up to me to tell me about his sister Kimberly that had been murdered a few years earlier. Kimberly had left her house to go shopping at a mall close to her home. She never returned home. This is her story.

Kim was in the parking lot when a young woman, Sharon, whom she had known from buying pot, approached her with a young man Kim didn't know by her side. Sharon asked Kim if she could give her and her boyfriend Gary a ride. Sharon told Kim that her car had broken down. Kim said sure, and this would change Kim's life and that of her family's lives forever.

Shortly after driving her car, Gary pulled a gun on Kim and forced her to get into the trunk of her car. Kim's mother had bought her and her brother a red fire extinguisher after watching a car catch

142

on fire, to keep in the trunk of their car. Kim used the red fire extinguisher to hit the trunk's door to try and escape. Kim kept beating the trunk, making loud noises, and upsetting the two kidnappers driving the stolen car. The couple had been up for three days on drugs.

Kim's car ran out of gas. The couple pulled Kim's car over to the side of the road and flagged down a man in a pickup truck to ask for help. He got out of his truck to assist Sharon and her boyfriend, when he heard Kim beating the trunk of her car and screaming for help.

He said to the two kidnappers, "What's going on? Why is there a girl screaming in the trunk of your car?"

Gary pulled his gun on the man and told him to open the trunk of the car. Then Gary turned to Sharon and asked her what should he do next?

Sharon said, "Shoot one!"

So Gary shot Kim right in front of the man they had pulled over. Then they forced the man at gun point to get into his truck and follow Sharon, who was driving Kim's car with Kim in the trunk. They dropped Kim's car off in a parking lot of the nearest apartment building, and then took the man hostage in his truck. The man knew their plan was to murder him also, because he was a witness to Kim's murder. It was only just a matter of time.

The man decided to jump out of the fast moving pickup truck. He broke his collarbone when he landed on the ground, but ran for his life into the trees. The pickup truck pulled over to the side of the road, sat there for a few minutes, then sped away down the street. The man ran to the nearest pay phone, called the police and waited for them to show up. He took the policemen to where Kim's body was stuffed in the back of her car. He helped draw a picture of the two murderers at the police station.

The two cold-blooded killers had gotten away. Nobody knew where they were, or where to even begin looking for them. Meanwhile the two murderers were in Mexico to stay low for a while. It wasn't long after that they got bored and decided it was safe to go back home to Houston.

Meanwhile, Wayne's mother and father's marriage was falling apart. They both blamed each other for Kim's death. Both parents were obsessed with finding Kim's killers, and Wayne was just left to fend for himself. His parents eventually got a divorce.

Wayne's mom decided to go to a famous psychic medium in Houston. Sylvia the psychic had short red hair and was a middle aged woman, about the same age as Wayne's mom. The Houston police department often used Sylvia to help solve murder cases. She would pray to Jesus to give her wisdom on her readings. A tape was used to record her readings and give to her clients.

Kim's reading went something like this: Sylvia said Kim knew her killers and that they would eventually be brought to justice. Sylvia said in her reading that she saw Kim inside her trunk hitting the inside of the trunk with something like a red piece of metal. It was the fire extinguisher that Kim's mom had bought for Kim shortly before her death. Sylvia spoke of personal things about Kim's life that only her mom could have known about. Kim was somehow connected with Sylvia on a different plane or level of consciousness to help comfort her mother's mind about her brutal death. Kim was reaching out to her mom to let her know that she was in God's hands and at peace.

I have never seen or met another human being as attuned to God and messages to the loved ones that are left behind to face life after the death of their loved ones as Sylvia was.

Eventually Kim's killers were caught and arrested for her murder. Sharon and Gary were pulled over for a traffic violation, and they had an outstanding warrant for their arrest. While in jail they were charged with the murder of Kim and the kidnapping of the truck driver because of their sketches. Sharon's father, a rich and successful doctor in Houston, posted bail for her until her trial date. The Houston Robbery Homicide Division made a deal with Sharon that if she would testify against her boyfriend, Gary, then murder charges would be dropped against her. She would just get probation. Kim's mom was shocked, because it was Sharon who had told Gary to kill Kim. Sharon was getting off scot free for first degree murder. The Houston police department wanted to make sure that Gary received the death penalty for Kim's death.

As the trial date finally arrived, Sharon took the witness stand and turned state's evidence against Gary. Gary was so devastated by Sharon's betrayal that when he took the stand to testify as to what happened to Kim, he said, "I killed Kimberly in cold blood and if I had it to do all over again, I *would* do it again."

Gary sealed his death sentence by threatening to kill every jury member and their family members if the jury didn't give him the death sentence. It didn't take long for the jury to find him guilty and sentence him to death row.

As Gary sat on death row waiting for his execution, he had a change of heart and decided he wanted to live. He had his lawyers start appealing his murder charges. His lawyers were trying to get all murder charges dropped against him, stating that the detectives had Sharon lie and give false testimony against him. Gary's love for Sharon had now turned into revenge and hate for her, as she freely moved on to start a new life. Kim's mom vowed to see that Gary be sentenced to death, but she had no say over Sharon's release.

Wayne became a lost soul dealing with not only the loss of his sister, but also the loss of his parent's attention. His parents were so consumed with getting justice for their daughter Kim that Wayne just kind of fell thru the cracks. It was such a hopeless tragedy for all Kim's family. The last I heard, Gary was still sitting on death row in Huntsville State Prison filing for an appeal to his death sentence.

DARLENE PRYOR

Darlene Pryor was born in Panama, in the Canal Zone. Growing up in a military family, she was fortunate to experience life both in Alabama and overseas in Germany. Darlene's educational background consists of a Bachelor's degree in Corrections with a minor in Sociology and a Master's degree in Public Administration. She believes that everyone has a story to tell. As a mother of five sons who is also a breast cancer survivor, she draws from her personal experiences to write of love, redemption, and restoration, with the intent of uplifting and encouraging her readers.

Darlene has completed her first novel entitled *Dreams of Tamar*, a compelling tale of a group of young Christian friends who learn the meaning of grace. She is currently engaged in the editorial process as she embarks on her second endeavor, *Dreams of My Father*.

Darlene Pryor currently resides in Lancaster, Ca.

TAMAR

This is a lady full of grace

Always with a smile on her face

Masking the pain and tears

Almost ready to reveal her fear

Rising to overcome

146

HIDDEN IN PLAIN SIGHT

When in a crowd, I'm more alone
than when I'm sitting here at home.

I look around but do not see
what all this has to do with me.

There must be more than what I see;
something that could set me free.

I'm sure that someday in a wink,

I will find the missing link.

He may be short, he may be tall,

He may not be a guy at all.

The reason that I do not see

What there is to set me free

May be that it's here inside of me.

IF I ASKED YOU

If I asked you to love me forever, could you?

If I asked you to love me tonight, would you?

If I asked you to hold me in your arms forever, could you?

If I asked you to hold me in your arms tonight, would you?

If I look into your eyes, will I see beyond tonight?

Is this love you've brought me a dream come true,
    or is it a fantasy?

I could love you forever, if you let me.

I could love you tonight, if you want me.

I could hold you forever, if you let me.

I would hold you tonight, if you want me.

If you look into my eyes you will see forever.

My love for you is not a dream; my love for you is not a fantasy.

Dreams don't always come true, and fairytales aren't real.

IF I COULD

It's been so long since we've seen each other eye to eye,
    so long since we've shared a night

I haven't heard your gentle laugh, nor seen your tender smile

Our little talks, our long, long walks, when we put
    our future plans in nature's hands

Stay on my mind all the time

And if I could bring back yesterday, I'd take us to the day we met

To when we felt we had infinite time to learn each other,
    though we hadn't yet

And if I could bring back the good times,
    I'd take us to the laughter

To when we enjoyed life just because we shared it,
    and nothing else mattered

And if I could bring back the love

I'd take us to the feelings we shared so deeply
    and openly filled with yearning,

That they were as natural as sunrise in the morning

And if I felt that you could answer just one thing,

I'd ask you...

Was yesterday too long ago?

Are the good times too far away?

Is the love really lost? (Three things)

And if I could plan the future I would have you say...

Yesterday is never too long ago

The good times are always near

And our love is always here

Then, I would hold you tight and keep you close...

If I could

LIFE AND PLUM TREES

Growing up in a military household one learns early that family is one of the most important factors in our lives. My father was a career service man (Army) and my family made several major moves during my youth. Our somewhat transient lifestyle lent itself to our becoming a rather close-knit bunch. As a child living in those circumstances one learns very early on that their immediate family is just about the only constant in their life.

See, I come from a large family. I am the fourth child and second daughter of six children: three sons and three daughters. There was never a time when I felt lonely or displaced. No matter where we moved, I always knew there would be at least one familiar face at our new school and another on the playground. I give my parents credit for making us feel that no matter where we were, if our family was together we were at home. My parents both grew up in rural Louisiana. Their children were born and raised from Anchorage, Alaska, to Panama in the Canal Zone.

As a young African American couple raising a family in the South during the sixties, my parents managed somehow to make it all seem effortless: raising and providing for a large family and relocating several times. I have to say that they were ahead of their time. My mother has worked outside of the home for as long as I can remember. She and my father both were always very active in all of our youthful endeavors: from coaching little league and serving as officers on the board of the American Youth Association, to chaperoning field trips.

Back in Alabama, the two of them would toil in their vegetable garden in the summer, and we would all help with picking and cleaning greens, or snapping peas. One year when my daddy was clearing land for the garden, my brother and I complained that he was killing the plum trees. He let us pick a couple of small trees to move up into the yard closer to our house. He told us we would have to water and nurture them until they were strong enough to grow on their own.

We started out diligently watering our little trees each day, watching to see that they were striving, and looking for fruit to appear. Soon we became disinterested in watching trees grow and would forget to water them.

One hot afternoon during a dry spell, my daddy called us around back. He asked us what happened to our trees. We had not even noticed they were dying. Daddy explained to us that we had taken on the responsibility of these two trees, and we could not turn our backs on them because they did not bear fruit as soon as we would have liked. He assured us that if we took good care of our trees they would eventually grow strong enough to strive on their own and give us plums sweeter than any we could find in the woods or even at the grocery store.

So we resumed caring for our trees. They did not bear fruit that first year but the next year we did have the best plums around. Daddy was right! Those plums tasted that much better because we knew our efforts had enabled those trees to grow and produce.

The experience with the fruit trees is just one example of my parents' many life lessons that I find myself referring to as I raise five sons of my own. I often ask how my parents were able to make it all seem so easy. My mother explained to me that it was never easy.

"You just get your priorities in order, get up and do what you have to do and don't sweat the small stuff. The most important thing you can remember each morning is: if you wake up, it's a good day."

It took me a while, but today I kind of think I get the message.

THEY SAID VS. HE SAID

they said I was too weak, some even said I was too small

He said: His strength is in my weakness

they said I couldn't fight, some even said I already lost

He said: The battle is not mine

they said the road to success was dark and winding, some even
said impassable

He said: He will make my crooked paths straight

they said the doors would not open, some even said
they were locked

He said: He will open doors no man can close

they said I'd never make it, some even said I'd fail

He said: I've already won

they said my past was checkered, some even said it was
shameful

He said: my latter days will be greater than my former

they said I wasn't special, some even said I was nobody

He said: I am the daughter of the King

they said I'm just a girl from nowhere, some even said
I didn't deserve success

He said: I am blessed and highly favored

they said my past is my destiny, some even said my past
is who I am

He said: I am HIS

Enough said!

I AM TAMAR

I am not a weeping willow nor a shrinking violet.

Many have tried to break my spirit,

No matter what life has brought against me,

My spirit remains intact and my will remains strong.

I am like butter that has been beaten and whipped into cream.

And cream always rises to the top.

I am a palm tree.

Storms may rage against me, and fierce winds may blow,

I sway back and forth, and I may even bend.

But I never, ever, break.

I am Tamar.

DARRELL MONTGOMERY

Darrell Montgomery was born in Oregon. A strong work ethic was instilled in him from age twelve when he worked as a paperboy. At seventeen he began working in a saw mill and later moved on to logging. His memories of his early years now provide material for writing stories - like when he saved enough money to buy and cruise around in a 1948 Cadillac, or when he met and married his sweetheart, Anita, still his sweetheart sixty-one years later. They have three children, two boys and a girl.

Besides the lumber business, Darrell worked in the sign business off and on for fifty years. He also spent twenty-two years with Lockheed. All this time he had an interest for writing, because he realized that art and sign work also tell a story. For example, he put the NASA logo on the tail of an SR-71 Blackbird, and that is story material in itself. Darrell, now retired, joined the Antelope Valley Writers Association at the suggestion of a friend, and has now published his first story.

LIFE AT THE END OF THE TUNNEL

In 1947, I lived in West Fir, Oregon, a lumber mill town on the North Fork of the Willamette River. The nearby town of Oakridge, where I was attending high school, was founded long ago when wagon trains took pioneers westward. It had, over time, transformed into a Southern Pacific railroad town supplying lumber critical to the war effort and then to the housing boom for the returning GI's and their families.

One day my friend, Bob, and I stayed after school for basketball practice only to realize that we couldn't hitch a ride home to West Fir on the other side of the ridge. This left us with three options, all of which involved walking: (1) over the ridge, more like a mountain, a real hike; (2) around the ridge, following the road seven miles which would take awhile; or (3) through the 2000 foot train tunnel. The tunnel was built in 1901 and went through the ridge between the two towns.

We agreed and chose the latter to save our feet, already tired from basketball. The odds of a train coming through in the next ten minutes were slight. The entrance to the tunnel was constructed of three-foot blocks of cement that stair-stepped thirty feet out and up to the mouth of the opening. The tunnel was cased with cement and vertical timber to the bedrock.

We could actually see the end of the tunnel, but only as a vertical slit of light because the whole thing had been dug with a slight curve to it. As we walked through, we could only see that slit and the light from it glancing off the two shiny rails that we stayed between. We were three-quarters of the way through when we heard the echoing of the crossing bells as they started clanging at the homeward end.

As we both began to run I wondered which way the train was coming. A glance over my shoulder confirmed my fears; it was the Number 20 passenger train, and though we were closer to the far side of the tunnel than the train, there was a downhill grade that gave more advantage to the train's speed than our own. At this point, I considered hugging the wall while the train went past, but remembered the almost tragic incident that had happened years before when the train stalled in the tunnel, almost asphyxiating everyone on board.

I passed Bob. Then I tripped and fell down. Then Bob fell on me. We scrambled to our feet; it was now easier to see the light of the engine illuminating our every stride. We veered right as we exited the tunnel; I can still hear the raw power of the engine pounding its way toward us. I felt the twisting in my gut as it focused all of its might to my straining legs, and the unparalleled relief after emerging just feet ahead of this relentless smoke belching, fire breathing beast.

Fifty years later I received a package from Bob and in it was a belt buckle with the image of one of those great black beauties, and a note saying, "We're still here. Love, Bob."

ERLINDA C. MOODY

Erlinda Moody was born on March 21, 1947, in San Bernardino, California. Growing up in 'Berdoo' in a Mexican American family provided Linda with many colorful stories based on culture and history, as well as unique characters she encountered throughout her youth. Along with her parents and siblings, their contributions provided the color and design to a fabric which was robust with pride, determination, humor, and most of all, love.

Having moved to Palmdale, California, Linda yearned to continue her passion for writing. She found the Antelope Valley Writers Association comprised of what she describes as "the best group of writers I know." She considers herself very lucky to be among others who share her passion for storytelling, but most all, she is grateful for the new friendships she has formed. She thanks her writing group for the encouragement, and urges all to be ready to "tell a story."

THE BRIDE DOLL

One summer when I was about eight years old, I remember going with my family *a las uvas*. We headed north to Fresno, California, to pick grapes. The money made from this stoop labor was to be used to get ahead of bills and for our clothes in the fall when school resumed. All this was done with a determination. This was extra money.

This particular summer, we went ahead of my father who stayed behind until he got his two weeks' vacation from Santa Fe. Then he would head north to join us for two weeks of hot sun, sweat, and dirt.

We would stay in tents on the property that belonged to a farmer whose grape crop we picked. I used to hate going to Fresno. How I would cry when I would look at the long rows of grapes. So many grapes. *Habia tantas uvas.* There were so many grapes.

At the end of the week, all of us would pile into the car and go to a little store to pay on the provisions that had been charged during the week. Every Friday, in a hypnotic walk, I would go to the back of the store and stare at the top of the meat counter.

You see, there was a bride doll on the counter that would beckon to me each time I walked through the store's door. I'd stand in front of it until I was called by my mother to come because we were leaving. I still looked back at the doll.

Oh, how I wished my father would buy me that doll. I never dared ask for the doll because even at that age, I knew it was a luxury we couldn't afford. I never let the words out of my mouth, but I would grab my father's hand and say, *"Mira, que bonita la mona papa!"* - "Look at how beautiful the doll is Papa."

And he would reply, *"No, no tenemos dinero."* - "No, we do not have any money." And I would keep standing there imagining the doll in my arms.

Finally, the time came for us to leave Fresno and return home, and we made a last stop at the store to pay for what we owed. I went to the counter for one last look and my heart fell to my feet. My doll was gone! Someone had bought her. I was crushed.

My father called us to get in the car, and I started to cry. My older brother began to make fun of me. As I sat down in the car, my father handed me a box. Inside the box was my bride doll.

I recall everything about that day. I held the doll in the box all the way home. When I got home, I ran to my friend's house to show her off, of course still in the box. I didn't want her touched.

When I finally took her out of the box, she was on display for months. As time went on, I washed her hair and all of her hair went straight. I took off her clothes and she wore original designer clothes. I was the designer.

This doll to me was a sacrifice made to make a child happy. At that age, what did I know about life? How long had my father sweated under the sun for the money to buy that doll for me? He used money that could have gone for groceries, gas, and many other things, but he had spent it on the bride doll for me because I had my heart set on it.

THE FERRY BOAT SERENADE

As we stood on the hard, hot, and dusty road we could see the yellow school bus in the distance, taunting us. My friend Lila and I had missed the yellow bus that would take us away from the groves of walnuts waiting in the burning sun to be picked by our parents, away from the migrant camp where we lived during the harvest season, and away to a big school with many children.

School was a red brick building. There were many books in the library we could hold in our hands and be transported to special places. In our classroom, we could draw with crayons that were the colors of the rainbow. A merry-go-round and swings waited on the playground. We played on them during recess. So many wonderful things were ours for those few precious hours we were at school.

The best part of school was that we were pupils in our first grade teacher's class. She was a beautiful woman with blonde hair that reminded me of shimmering gold. She was tall, yet graceful in her movements. Her voice was always soft like a gentle breeze in the cool of the evening after the sun goes down. I liked to believe she was part angel. She was very kind, and always made us feel that we were part of her class. In no way would we ever do anything to disappoint her.

I looked at Lila and we both started to run after the bus as it traveled on the road through the fields. As we ran, we fell time and again yelling at the top of our lungs, "Wait for us! *Esperen nos!* Don't leave us! *No nos dejen!*" We ran that morning a little over three miles which seemed like twenty miles.

Finally, and out of breath, we reached the school. Since we were only eight years old, both of us imagined horrible consequences. Maybe we would be thrown out. We had to think up a good excuse. A very good excuse had to be thought up for our appearance.

We were two small Mexican girls, covered in dirt and with wild, uncombed hair. We agreed to say we were late because our camp had caught fire and burned, which was partly true. There had been a fire the night before when the dryer that was used to process the walnuts had burned. Many workers lost their belongings. The little they had worked for in the long days was gone overnight.

When we reached the classroom, the teacher asked why we were late. It didn't take us a second to answer before the story of the fire of the century was told. We poured out the story, adding more and more details, making it a huge disaster.

Seeing us in such a state, and knowing we were poor, our teacher quickly took us to the principal's office and retold our tale to a gathering of white, middle class staff members. Lila and I stood together, holding hands and not knowing what to do. They stared at us as if expecting us to do something. As the minutes passed, I said nervously in my small voice, "Lila and I want to sing you a song."

"A song?" they asked.

"Yes, a song," I replied. Without wasting any time, our arms around each other's waists, we began to sing:

> "I love to ride a ferry-boat
> where the music is so merry
>
> There's a girl that plays the concertina
>
> In the room and upper deck arena
>
> Where boys and girls are dancing,
>
> Where sweethearts are romancing.
>
> Life is like a Mardi Gras.
>
> *Funiculla, funiculla"*

As I look back now that I am sixty-four years old, I can vividly remember the incident as if only yesterday. I was still that little girl. So scared in a world alien to me, yet wanting so much to be accepted, and not knowing what to do to gain that acceptance that was so necessary at the moment. Lila and I gave what we had. It was only a simple song, yet we presented it like a valuable offering, and to us it was.

Lila and I sang the whole song. When we finished, everyone clapped. Our principal went to the upper-drawer of his desk and took out a box of lollipops. The lollipops were sold at the school for a nickel a piece. Neither Lila nor I ever had a nickel to buy one, but now the principal was actually giving us a lollipop.

We quickly grabbed the candy, and licked the sweet taste very slowly. This was the trophy for our duet. This was the gesture that meant 'you are not in trouble for coming late to school.' That afternoon as we rode on the bus, our angelic teacher rode on the bus with us. She had bags of clothing for us and wanted to give it to our parents. I felt as if my small heart would burst from love and pride as I looked at my beautiful teacher walking by my side into our camp of burnt tents, old cars, and tired occupants.

The next day, Lila and I waited for the bus. Oh, we were never late to school again. That day Lila had a new used red dress with ribbons to match, and I had a jumper with a safety pin pattern. Never will I forget this incident when we were left behind by the school bus. The day we thought the worst would happen had been turned around by a teacher who could see no color distinction, loved children, and wanted the best for her students - all of them.

THE WRATH OF GRAPES

As I looked through the car window, I could see my father standing at the curb with a sad look on his face. He was waving goodbye to us as the car caravan of Mexican gypsies started down the street. We went to Fresno in the summer time to pick the grape crop in order to make extra money for the months ahead. This money would be used for school clothes, shoes and the little extras my father's pay check could not cover.

I cried as I was told to get in the car. I'm a cry-baby anyway and have always had a tremendous hatred for picking grapes. Filled with dread, I could look forward to a vacation from hell.

The caravan was made up of two cars. Both of the cars were literally on their last wheels. My Uncle Dicky was driving the car in front of ours. It was loaded down with tents, utensils, and food. Inside the car were my mother, who was pregnant, my brother, Aunt Aurora and her son, Richard Jr. Also in the car was my mother's picture of the Virgin de Monte Razo that she carried in her lap.

My mother's religious faith in this particular saint was one of total devotion. The Virgin's picture had a small altar in the corner of my parent's bedroom. With rosaries and a lit candle, my mother held silent vigils in front of the picture. To this Virgin went only the most important petitions. Anything else could be left behind, but not her picture of the Virgin.

My Uncle John was the driver of our car. Inside this car were my grandmother, my sister, and myself. Our car was also heavily packed with clothes, blankets, tools, and food. The cars, with all of us in them, looked like something out of the movie *Tobacco Road*. What articles didn't fit inside the cars, were tied on the roof and on the back top of the trunks. Other families went to the beach or mountains, but ours, you could say, was a real outdoor adventure in the first homemade recreational vehicles.

We traveled several hours, finally reaching the two-lane highway that was halfway between our destinations. The road was uphill and through high mountains. We were nearing the top of the mountain, when the cars started to heat up. To this day, I wonder how the trip was even attempted. *A quien se le ocure.* Who would have thought? Necessity can do strange things to you, especially when you are trying to get ahead in the right way, by doing an honest day's work.

The caravan had to stop on the side of the road in order to let our cars cool down before resuming our journey. My Uncle Dicky parked his car about twenty feet in front of ours. My Uncle John parked the car we were in on a steep incline. Rocks were put behind the tires to prevent the cars from rolling back. My grandmother was asleep in the front seat. My sister and I were asleep in the back seat.

All of a sudden, the car started to roll off the steep mountainside. When my Uncle Dicky saw the car slowly falling over the side, his first reaction was to run towards the car without a thought that he was risking his life. He ran *como el Superman Mexicano* and dove into the car to pull the brake. My grandmother, quick thinker that she was, pulled him through the car window - mind you, as the car was turning. Not to be left out of this excitement, my mother jumped out of the parked car in front and yelled at the top of her lungs, "*Virgin de Monte Razo, salva los!*" - "Virgin de Monte Razo, save them!" All the while, my Aunt Aurora was pulling her hair, and my brother and cousin were jumping up and down, crying and screaming.

In the car, I remember turning upside down over and over. Eggs and tortillas are flying through the air as the car continued to roll down the ravine. Believe it or not, *pero lo juro*, I swear we must have fallen at least one hundred and fifty feet. The amazing thing was that we landed right side up. If we had landed upside down, I'd either be playing *la harpa con los angelitos* right now, or have a bad case of sunburn or should I say burnt feet from stepping on hot coals. If there is such a thing as *milagros* or miracles, this was one the Virgin answered because of my mother's faith and belief in her.

We got out of the car without a scratch, and loaded ourselves up with what we could carry. As we started to climb up the ravine, the car burst into flames.

The reality of the seriousness of this incident did not occur to me until years later when I recalled what happened. We could all have been resting in peace.

Do you think for a moment this incident stopped us? *Nel.* No. *Nunca.* Never. *Nos dimos fuerza.* It gave us strength. With the determination of our Aztec, Toltec, and Mixtec cultures, we did not give up in the face of defeat. Onward we continued.

We all relished in our miraculous saving by praying a rosary on the embankment; we then piled into Uncle Dicky's car and sped onward with a stronger determination than ever to make it to the promised land of grapes and dirt.

We, children and adults, survived the struggles - heat, dirt, no hot water. We made it from payday to payday, took showers with a garden hose, and slept in beds made out of boxes of grapes. We sold bottles to go to the public swimming pool. The rancher's children threw rocks and called us names.

There are so many things I could tell you about. Listening to me you might think we missed out on a lot by not having enough money and having to struggle. But before making such a decision, you would also have to hear me say that out of these experiences came strength and a belief in ourselves to not give up no matter what struggles lay ahead.

We cement our past with our memories. *No nos damos.* We did not give in. *Nunca.* Never.

HILDA TARAZI

Hilda Tarazi was born in Palestine and lived there until she was sixteen. She went to the private Friends Girls' School and learned English. She speaks fluent Arabic and taught at a boys' school. In 1948 she left everything behind and moved with her family to Iraq then to Syria. After migrating to the United States, she worked as a bilingual aid and secretary in Dearborn, Michigan. Upon retirement she moved to California and worked in schools in San Diego then Lancaster.

Hilda has written articles for the *Washington Report on Middle East Affairs* in a special commemorative issue about the Nakba of 1948, and how her family left their home. She has also written a vegetarian cookbook called *Palestinian Kitchen* and co-authored another called *Sahtein*, Arabic for "eat with good health." Besides her writing endeavors, she has grandchildren and great grandchildren who give her joy in her later years.

COMING TO AMERICA

My family and I were living in Palestine when our names came on the Quota list to come to America. At the time we were in the city of Ramallah which means "land of God." The idea was very exciting because in America they have freedoms which we didn't have in my country like riding a bicycle, roller skating and ice skating, swimming, and driving a car.

My thoughts took me further. I would become a movie star in Hollywood because I loved acting and sing from watching American musical movies. Because of those movies I could put myself in the roll of the actor and would provide the education of children for now and the future. So many movies were based on the lives of teachers that encouraged the education of those in need.

My husband was reluctant to leave, so we had to take a vote. My four young children all agreed and voted with me to take this opportunity. My sisters and parents were already there. They had described America to us as beautiful with many, many opportunities to excel in life doing whatever we had dreamed about. We could further our education, have a business, and be happy.

The actual description of America was that money was growing on trees. We pictured that in our heads, but knew the true meaning was that we could earn money by hard work and knowledge.

What to take with me on the plane was a chore. I came from a small town and there were no shops or malls for ready-made clothes. The only way was to copy styles and sew our own clothes. I was from a family with more money than most, and my clothes were handmade by seamstresses based on styles from catalogs. We used the Sears Catalogs that had been brought to us from people that had come from America. My sister told me not to bring any clothes as the shops were full of nice, ready-made clothes to fit. I found out later that they didn't fit as well as the clothes which we had made for us but the styles were certainly an improvement.

We bought our tickets to America and the idea of stopping in Paris and London was very appealing to us. We didn't know anyone in Paris but did have my brother and his family nearby who we could visit with so we scheduled our stop. He took us on a tour and showed us the old castles and palaces. To us we liked them but the Wax Museum seemed to stand out. We saw famous people there like the Queen of England, Mohammad Ali the boxer, King Hussein of Jordon, and Michael Jackson who looked very real. We were also attracted to the slot machines. My brother encouraged us to save our money and so we did.

Everything was strange and different for us and we wanted to explore everything. We did bring gifts from the Holy Land. We gave gold bangle bracelets to my brother's wife. His four-year-old son cried when we gave him a gold cross. We found out he wanted one with the crucifix on it.

Certainly the life style was different. We had always warmed our milk. They drank it cold. We were asked what we wanted for breakfast. At home we put everything we had on the table and each chose what he wanted so there was no waste. There we saw food wasted all the time. People ate a few bites and threw the rest away. We stayed with my brother for a week and enjoyed the visit very much.

We arrived in New York on October 31st and stayed with a cousin overnight and didn't tour. It was Halloween. Can you imagine what went through our minds that day? The kids loved the candy part. Our final destination was Washington DC to see my parents who welcomed us with open arms.

The next day we went to get our social security cards and to look for a job. We couldn't get a government job because we weren't citizens. What is there in Washington DC that is not a government job? My sister in Detroit called us to welcome us and said there were more opportunities there for non-English speaking people to work in the auto industry on the assembly line. Off we went.

It was tough looking for a job without a car. My husband walked a block to take the bus downtown in freezing weather. We finally rented a house and day by day we adapted to the American life.

My husband got a job with the Ford Motor Company as an accountant in the main office building, and I worked in the Dearborn public school system as a bilingual teacher assistant and a secretary. Detroit was a good move for us and a good opportunity. I learned to drive a car, and we had just one. I would drop my husband off at his office and then go to school.

We were excited at our first Christmas approaching. We bought presents and put them in our car and moved on to the next store. When we came out with our arms full, our car was open and all the presents in it were gone.

Our children did okay in school but would have been top of their class if back home. The schools are different and their minds were on other things. They got ideas from other students and did what they pleased. As teenagers they worked in fast food restaurants and spent their money on motorcycles and cars. They finally did get on track, but it took them longer to finish their education.

As for us, we did live the American way. We bought a home, learned to skate and swim, and stayed in Detroit till we both retired. We then moved to California.

America is beautiful, land of the free and land of opportunities. I am glad I came here.

MELINDA M. HUNTER

Melinda Hunter, a transplant from Oak Park, Illinois, now calls the high desert of Southern California her home. She is an active member of the Antelope Valley Writers Association and has been writing poetry since she was five. Melinda has a B.A. degree from Carleton College in English and holds a M.Div. degree from North Park Seminary in Chicago. She has one son who also lives in the Antelope Valley.

Melinda enjoys writing poetry and short stories, and has created a number of stories with the main character being her adventurous cat, Oro. She is also tackling her first novel entitled *The Fifth Jesus*.

DESERT DIAMONDS

Sparkling on the dead branch

Tiny jewels like diamonds glisten.

It rained last night in the desert.

As the drops descended

   they fastened themselves

   to the bare branches

   and created

This astounding beauty!

THE FIFTH JESUS (An Excerpt)

(This story is an excerpt from Melinda Hunter's book in progress entitled, *The Fifth Jesus*, which she hopes to have completed in 2016.)

You have to realize that I was totally out of my mind when I found myself in Dr. Schwartz's office. I thought I was Jesus, and as Jesus, I had complete power over the world and everyone in it.

"She needs to be admitted," said Dr. Schwartz to my husband. Jack looked perplexed and shocked.

"Are you sure?"

"Absolutely," responded the doctor. "I want you to take her to Lakeside Hospital, where I am on the staff. I'll let them know you are coming."

DAY 1:

I was shaking and my thoughts were racing. *If I am Jesus, why am I nervous?* We took the elevator up to the psych ward on the fourth floor. While Jack talked to the nurse in charge, another nurse led me to a table where a group of patients were playing Monopoly.

"Why don't you watch, Melanie?" the nurse said kindly.

I HAD to watch. As Jesus, I was terrified. The fate of the world was there on that board. If I moved any piece, I could blow up everyone! The hotel on Boardwalk could be full of explosives. I sat there grasping my hands together; my whole body trembled.

A large woman with a green velvet turban on her head walked into the room. "I am the Queen of Egypt, Cleopatra," she announced grandly. "Call me Your Royal Highness," she added and then staring at me asked, "Who are you?"

"I'm Jesus," I replied.

Just then a long-haired bearded man in a bathrobe who was playing the table game with us stood up. "You can't be Jesus," he proclaimed. "I am the *real* Jesus!"

"What!" I exclaimed. *If he is Jesus, who am I?*

A male nurse came up to the table. "Come with me," he said. He took me down a hallway and into a room with a bed.

"Turn over," he ordered brusquely. Taking a huge needle, he gave me a shot in the buttocks. "You'll feel better now," he announced.

Better? The shot hurt a lot! However, the effects of it soon numbed my senses and I collapsed on the bed. A couple of minutes later, Jack came into the room. "I have to go now, Lilly," he said. 'Lilly' is my middle name, a pet name which he called me.

"Okay," I mumbled. By that time the shot had taken effect and I was groggy.

He kissed me and said, "I'll come back during visitor's hours and bring you some clothes.

Meanwhile, with the help of another nurse, I took off my street clothes and put on a hospital gown.

"Let's find you a room, sweetie," said the kind nurse.

"Fine." I was so groggy I could hardly stand.

"Why don't you lie down here," she suggested. "Supper is at 5:30."

The nurse woke me up for dinner and helped me out to the table. I ate in a zombie-like state, returned to my room, and collapsed. Weeks of not eating and sleeping had left me mentally and physically exhausted. Of course, the fact that I was Jesus should have brought me comfort but instead it only scared me. I couldn't handle that I had so much power.

Jack did come back during visitor's hours; however, I was totally out of it. He left some clothes and told the nurse he would be back the next day. So, thus ended Day One—my first of many in the psych unit.

DAY 2:
"Morning comes early and bright with dew. . ." (old lyric, author unknown)

In the psych unit we couldn't sleep in. There was no bugle reveille, but the nurse came around and woke us up.

"Up and at 'em," she said, standing at the door until we got out of bed. It was 6:30 a.m. Still groggy from the shot and the other meds I had taken the night before, I opened one eye.

"Breakfast is served," she said. "You can wear your hospital gown to breakfast."

I stumbled out, wearing my blue and white gown decorated with triangles which tied at the neck. My fellow 'inmates' were seated at long tables. I spotted Cleopatra. She beckoned me to come sit by her. Today, she wore a fancy blue turban fastened with two gold clips.

"Dahling," she said, "you look fab!"

"Fab?" I exclaimed, "This is my hospital gown!" Then, being more alert, I got into the spirit and said, "Thank you, Cleopatra, I dressed up since I knew you would be at breakfast. I have to look my best in such famous company." Since she and the other Jesus were the only two people I knew, I agreed to sit with them.

"How is everything in Egypt?" I queried.

"Egypt--well the natives are restless. I am trying to quell an uprising."

"Oh my, I am sorry to hear that," I said, not really meaning it.

Without further conversation we ate our breakfast which consisted of hot cereal, juice, orange slices and a banana. I was not hungry, but ate out of force of habit.

"ART ACTIVITY," announced the nurse. She shepherded us into a large, sunny room. There was a kiln and many pieces of painted and unpainted greenware on the shelves. Garish paintings with wild colors hung around the room. We sat down at large tables. The art therapist was a woman with a strong accent of some sort. I found out that she was Hungarian and her name was Aliz. Her assistant was a beautiful, blonde woman in her early thirties named Penny. Both women, as I experienced, were passionate about art and also passionate about helping us mentally ill patients regain our health through working at the art projects.

During the art session, I met a young woman named Deborah. Deborah, like me, was diagnosed with postpartum depression. She had long dark hair, brown eyes and the saddest face that I had ever seen. She had been in the psych unit for over a week. Every evening during visitor's hours, her husband came to visit. He often brought flowers or some other gift. Even when he was present, Deborah's sad expression never changed. As ill as I was, I felt sorry for her. Her baby, a daughter, was almost two months, the same age as my son, Jackie. I asked Deborah about her child. She mumbled something back that I could hardly understand.

I hadn't seen my baby since I had entered the hospital. My mother-in-law was keeping him at her house. She had hired a nanny to come in during the daytime since she was a teacher. My husband went to his mom's three times a week to help feed little Jackie.

About 2 p.m. Dr. Schwartz came into the ward to see his patients. The nursing staff flocked around him, eager to do his bidding. We patients were not allowed to stay in our rooms, but had to be out in the common area, talking to the other patients or reading. I was sitting in a chair, holding a book, but not really reading it. The doctor came up to me and sat down nearby.

"Mrs. Hooper," he said, "I hear you went to art therapy this morning."

"Yes," I answered.

"How was it?"

"I started painting some ceramic bookends."

"Good. I want you to go every day. I am adjusting your medications so you will feel less depressed," he told me. "I talked to Jack today and to your brother-in-law, Barry," he continued. "Barry is explaining to your in-laws about the severity of your illness."

My brother-in-law was a doctor, and although a pathologist, he understood depression due to his training.

After Dr. Schwartz left, the time dragged. Irma, a.k.a. Cleopatra, came over and sat down beside me. "So you are Jesus," she scrutinized me carefully. "You need to know there are four others here who think they are Jesus. And you're the fifth. Guess you'll have to duke it out." She laughed.

"I am just tired and depressed today," I told her. "That guy who was playing the game, Jim, he even looks a little like him with his brown hair and brown beard, but I am THE ONE!!" I pronounced.

"When I was admitted here," Irma continued, "I told them I was Cleopatra. That's why I wear the turban on my head. Most of the time I'm just like you, tired and depressed. The medication slows you down so you can't think straight. It's for your own good, though," she sighed. "However, when I am Cleopatra, I feel less depressed. I feel so powerful! The doctor tells me that keeping up the delusion is making me worse, so he continues to confront me to give it up. He's threatening to try regression therapy on me."

"What is that?" I asked.

Just then a large man rolled up to us in a wheelchair. He was blonde and weighed over 250 pounds. Instead of clothes, he had a couple of towels fastened around his bottom to simulate a diaper. He also wore a t-shirt and carried a plastic baby bottle.

171

"Hi Dave," I said. I had met Dave in art therapy. "Why are you wearing a diaper?"

"Dr. Schwartz put me into regression therapy. He won't release me until I prove I'm ready to grow up." the large man replied.

"That's why you are in a wheel chair?" questioned Irma.

"Yes," replied Dave. "He makes you go back to infancy, and won't release you until you show him you are ready to grow up."

Little did I know that the same fate awaited me during my stay.

It was almost dinner time. My second day in the psych unit was almost over. I sat next to Deborah. Her head was lowered. I tried to talk to her, but she only mumbled something indistinguishable. Dave was next to me. A nurse was feeding him with a baby spoon.

"That's a good boy, Davie," she cooed in baby talk.

"Do something, Dave," urged Irma.

Finally, Dave yelled out, "I don't like this at all." He took the plastic food dish and threw it on the floor. We all applauded. The nurse came over and told Dave that he could return to his room, put on street clothes, and eat normally.

A few minutes later, Dave returned on foot, not in a wheelchair.

"Congratulations, Dave," I said, and everyone else entered in their good wishes except Deborah. She just sat in a chair, head down. I prayed silently that something would bring her back to health. After the excitement with Dave, I went back to my room.

At 7:00 p.m. sharp, Jack came to find me. "Do you want to sit out in the main room," he asked. "How was your day?"

"Okay, we had art therapy, lunch, I saw Dr. Schwartz, and then we had dinner."

"I went down to my parents' house last night," said Jack. "Our son is a darling little boy. I stay up at night three times a week to feed him."

"I'm glad," I said. "I'm really tired, Jack. I think it's the meds."

"Do you want me to leave?" he asked.

"Yes," I said.

"I love you, Lilly," he said. "I am praying constantly for your recovery." He kissed me softly and walked out.

DAY 3:
"If It's Tuesday, This Must Be Belgium," (Title of 1969 film directed by Mel Stuart).

I was still adjusting to the unit's schedule and the food. We had little or no physical activity. The patients who were a little better in health, sometimes went outside for a walk. It was October, so the weather was pleasant. All I could do was look out the window for now.

The hospital was in a highly populated area of Chicago not far from Lake Michigan, and tall apartment buildings and a few trees were all we could see from the windows. I could look out at the people below, the women pushing baby strollers, wrapped up in scarves and hats because of the wind off the lake, men and women walking quickly to their destinations. Oh yes, I recalled my baby was with my mother-in-law. Though I couldn't focus on him now. I could barely focus on the unit's activities, let alone a baby.

DOREEN KENNEDY

Doreen Kennedy grew up in a steel mill town outside of Pittsburgh, Pennsylvania. She has since lived all around the U.S.

It was the aerospace industry that brought the Kennedy family from green and rainy Atlanta, Georgia, to desert dry Palmdale, California. At first it was quite an adjustment for Doreen. She sought people who had the same interests and discovered a small writers group at a local library. Now called the Antelope Valley Writers Association, she helped it grow from several members to over thirty. Doreen also compiled and published the group's three anthologies, and established their non-profit status so funds from anthology sales could be donated to local charities.

Doreen considers education as the key to a successful life. After a twenty-five year career as a technical writer, she returned to college and received her degree in English, Secondary Education, with a minor in Professional Writing. Her goal is to get everyone, young and old, to enjoy writing.

CITY RAIN

Take off your clothes

and dance naked in the puddles

as the sky smiles rain

upon the children of the street.

Sweet summer rain

washes the city dust from the bricks

out of the cracks in the sidewalks

but never out of my soul.

A SNOW STORY

It was the day after Christmas and another beautiful day in Southern California, but without the usual crystal clear desert sky. There were clouds. Not the gray, threatening type that typically creep over the mountains when a storm is approaching, these resembled a field covered in a fresh blanket of snow. How I wanted to flip that sky upside down so I could roll in the cloud snow, like a stupid kid again, joyfully oblivious.

Instead I went inside and watched *White Christmas* for about the 180th time. Bing Crosby and Rosemary Clooney never sounded so good thanks to our new home theater system with five-speaker surround sound. I watched it all the way to the best part, the ending with all that snow. I knew it was just the fake Hollywood manufactured kind, but the 1080-pixel backlit LEDs made the white stuff look almost real as it drifted down the 60-inch flat screen. Maybe they should redo *White Christmas* in 3D? Who am I kidding? No amount of pixels or virtual reality can replace the thrill of being a child playing in the real stuff.

Snow, snow, snow, snow. My mind remains stuck in snow. So I shall pass my snow thoughts on to you.

Sadly, for so many adults a new snow equates to misery. Slipping and sliding on sidewalks, skidding on the roads. Shoveling the driveway, scraping the windshields. Can't get to work. Can't go to the store. Can't even order a pizza. Not to mention the next Ice Age and the probable end of the world as we know it.

But to kids, snow is heaven fallen from the skies complete with angels. It's snowballs and sledding and snowmen. Slipping, skidding, and sliding are all delightful things. And best of all, when it snows a lot - there's no school! Snow reminds me of all these things, but most of all it brings back my childhood.

I grew up in Pittsburgh, Pennsylvania, where the winters are cold and wet, the way winter should be for kids. Our town was born of coal and steel, and most of the year a gray ash filled the air. The mill dust coated everything in sight, turning the brick buildings and the tiny row houses that lined the streets into a landscape sketched in charcoal.

That is until winter. And then it would snow. All of a sudden my dark, dingy surroundings gleamed like porcelain. The roof tops, the steps, the cars, the sidewalks. Everything white! Streets became arrays of snow bumps where the cobblestones used to be. Even the trash cans in the alleys sparkled.

I was always the first one up and out the door - to christen the new fallen snow. It was a right I declared as mine, to make the first footprints even if it meant getting up before sunrise.

I would walk for a mile, maybe two, then walk back toward home retracing my original footprints, all the while taking in the immaculate transformation. It was a bonding - no, more than that - it was a confirmation, a renewal of my faith in the world by being a part of something so beautiful, even when it would last for only an hour or two. For the moment I was the snow queen dancing in my personal sea of white.

Soon the mob would awake - with their shovels and plows, and the cars with their chained tires, the salt and cinder trucks, and worst of all - the dogs.

The purity of it would be gone, but just until the next snowfall. And besides, even though befouled by adults and their machines, there was still all that snow to play in all day long.

BORROWED TIME

Eyes opened mind closed
eyes closed mind opened
win - lose
which to chose?

Don't weep don't cry
don't even try
to understand
what's not your hand.

Darkness surrenders
to morning sun.
The day is young
a song yet sung.

Don't worry be happy
Dance
ride a pumpkin to the ball.
Have some. Have it all.

Should have left long ago
but I'm here
for a reason -
so some say.

What do they know
What do I care
I just bide my time
on someone else's dime.

NAMES

I knew him as Dad. My mother always called him "Nay" His friends, co-workers, acquaintances, and even his own family members - well they called him "Charlie." I never knew where that came from until one day at one of many family gatherings I heard my Aunt Lou (his older sister) call him Charlie and I asked her why. She said that his real name was "Aniello" and when it was time to register him for school, being the eldest child, she had to take him. Aunt Lou said she was so nervous that she couldn't remember how to spell his name, so she just wrote "Charlie" on the registration form. My Dad would always laugh when he heard that story. He finally told me that when he started school they shortened his name to the more Americanized, "Neal." And that during WWII his buddies in the Army would call him Charlie. He liked that name and just decided to keep using it.

The stories of my Dad's many names were funny at first, but later took a more serious tone. As an adult, I constantly bugged Dad that he deserved compensation from the Army since he lost his hearing in one ear during WWII. He was a tough, no-nonsense guy, my Dad, typical of many men of his era, and didn't take handouts from anyone. "It's not a handout," I tried to explain in vain. So I decided to look into the situation on my own. And that's when I discovered he had different first names on different official documents. Maybe that didn't matter in the 1940s, but in the overly technical computer age that we now live in, it would cause major problems.

Funny how years need to pass before you can truly understand why some things are. I couldn't fathom why anyone would not want to use their real name, that is until I recently began substitute teaching in public schools. I encountered students, many of Asian and Middle Eastern heritages, who would ask me to call them by a different name. "My name is Ming Tao, but please don't call me that," he whispered, "call me Joe." Sometimes students would come to me before I called attendance and beg me not to use the name on the roster —"please call me Julie" said a girl of Korean descent.

Then I realized just how much my father and other children of immigrants must have been taunted and teased because of their foreign-sounding names, and how much they desired to be accepted in their new homeland. And how after eighty years - nothing had changed.

V. S. ALEXANDER

V.S. Alexander is the late husband of Pat Alexander, and his unique art graces the cover of this book.

V.S. Alexander was born in Montenegro, on the Adriatic Sea, in 1933. He excelled in sports and wrote poetry at an early age. This sportsman/poet/artist escaped from that communist country at age fifteen and went to Germany. He was chosen to go to the 1952 Olympics in Finland and compete in the decathlon and shot put. He came to America to live in St. Louis, Missouri, where he worked for a couple of years. Los Angeles, California, was his next home.

In addition to painting, he created many mosaics and stained glass art works with a well-known artist. After awhile he went to Las Vegas and obtained a position in a hotel-casino. Soon, he met and married Pat Taylor, a showgirl at the time. The couple moved to Pat's hometown of Buffalo, New York, where they raised two beautiful daughters. After their girls were grown, the Alexanders retired to Florida. V.S. Alexander died there in 1993.

EXILE FROM PARADISE

Postpone the celebration, let the drums lay low.
Axiomatic visions of unborn fantasies are lost.
Empty arms of summer, like a cross without God.
 Golgotha revisited. Where has everybody gone?

The structure of centuries past, like tassel-less rye,
Praying in the wind. Headless, protruded, and bent.
Who is the quisling of the night? Night without moon.
The gods are angry. Full of vengeance and bile.
Jealous and vulgar. Accumulating fear.

All because I stole a song from paradise.
One that I wrote. All about you.

INDIVIDUAL COPYRIGHTS

THE END

The Antelope Valley Writers Association
thanks you for your support,
and hopes that you enjoyed the poetry and prose
of the many talented writers
who live in
the Antelope Valley of Southern California.